THE
"GREAT STRIKE"

PERSPECTIVES ON
THE 1902 ANTHRACITE
COAL STRIKE

ACKNOWLEDGMENTS

The Ohio State University Department of History
granted permission for this publication to print editorial
cartoons from 1902 from its website,
where an impressive collection of features
on the 1902 strike may be found at
http://www.history.ohio-state.edu/projects/coal/1902AnthraciteStrike/

Frank Whelan, a writer of historical feature stories for
The Morning Call in Allentown, Pennsylvania,
donated copies of newspaper stories about the strike.
These are now part of the permanent collection at the
Archives of the National Canal Museum.

COVER

President Theodore Roosevelt, Michael J. Hoban, Bishop of the
Diocese of Scranton, and John Mitchell in front of the rectory of
Holy Savior Church in Wilkes-Barre during the strike.
Courtesy of the Pennsylvania Anthracite Heritage Museum.

**Canal History and
Technology Press**

National Canal Museum
30 Centre Square, Easton, PA 18042-7743

Sponsoring Organizations for the 100th Anniversary Commemoration of the "Great Strike"

Luzerne County Community College
Luzerne County Historical Society
Pennsylvania Historical and Museum Commission and the
    Anthracite Museum Complex
Pennsylvania Humanities Council
Pennsylvania Labor History Society

Supporting Organizations for the 100th Anniversary Commemoration of the "Great Strike"

Borough of Coaldale
City of Scranton
Coal Region Book Nook
Delaware and Lehigh National and State Heritage Corridor
Greater Shenandoah Area Historical Society
History Alive!
Lackawanna County Historical Society
Lackawanna Heritage Valley Authority
Luzerne County Tourist Promotion Agency
Marywood University
National Canal Museum
Pennsylvania AFL-CIO
Pennsylvania State Education Association
Schuylkill County Historical Society
Schuylkill River Valley National Heritage Area
Times-Shamrock, Inc.
United Mine Workers of America

This program has been supported in part by the Pennsylvania Humanities Council, the federal-state partner of the National Endowment for the Humanities.

CONTENTS

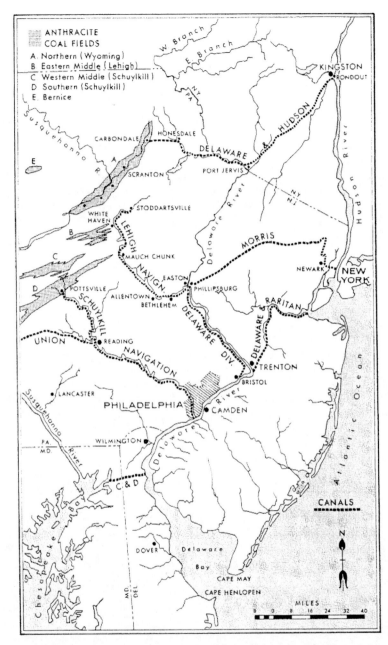

Map of Pennsylvania's anthracite regions, showing the coal fields and the canals that carried the coal to markets. In the second half of the century railroad networks were built to carry anthracite throughout the eastern United States. Anthracite became an essential fuel by the mid-19th century.

FOREWORD

"The Great Strike"
A 100th Anniversary Commemoration
of the 1902 Anthracite Coal Strike

Kenneth C. Wolensky,
Historian, Division of History
Pennsylvania Historical and Museum Commission

In the course of human affairs there is an inclination to view history as something that occurred somewhere else, as having been experienced by someone else. Recognizing that history includes people, places, and events, and the interpretation thereof in the broadest sense is a relatively contemporary phenomenon. Among the many public history functions of the Pennsylvania Historical and Museum Commission are to examine, interpret, and document the breadth and scope of the Commonwealth's past. One example of this work can be seen in the Commission's historical marker program. In the post-World War II era over 1,800 blue-and-gold historical markers have been dedicated around the Commonwealth in recognition of people, places, and events that have been influential in human history.

The anthracite coal strike of 1902 is among these events. During an era when Pennsylvania's "hard coal" commanded a significant share of the American energy market, over one hundred and fifty thousand mineworkers struck in May demanding higher wages, shorter workdays, more equitable weighing of coal, recognition of the United Mine Workers of America, and other concessions from coal operators. The strike shut down an industry vital to American commerce. It impacted workers, families, communities, and businesses dependent on coal and the income derived from it for their livelihoods. A contemporary equivalent might be if oil refinery workers in the eastern United States struck while consumers nevertheless demanded gasoline to fuel their vehicles and fuel oil to heat their homes.

As the fall of 1902 approached and supplies of hard coal for the coming winter months dwindled, President Theodore Roosevelt intervened and established the Anthracite Coal Strike Commission to adjudicate a settlement. With the encouragement of religious and union leaders, mineworkers agreed to return to work while the Commission conducted its investigation. At commission hearings in Scranton and in Philadelphia five hundred witnesses filled fifty-six volumes of testimony and described living and working conditions in the anthracite region. Discord was unmistakable. Attorney Clarence Darrow, representing the mineworkers, argued "they [coal operators] are fighting for slavery. We are fighting for freedom. They are fighting for the rule of man over man, for despotism, for darkness, for the past. We are striving to build up man." George Baer, president of the Philadelphia and Reading Coal and Iron Company, captured the sentiment of coal operators by arguing that "the rights and interests of the laboring man will be protected and cared for not by the labor agitators but by the Christian men of property to whom God has given control of the property rights of this county."

In March 1903, the Commission granted a ten percent wage increase, a nine-hour workday, new rules for the weighing of coal, establishment of a permanent board to adjudicate operator-worker disputes, and other concessions. That the federal government intervened in the strike established a precedent solidified in 1913 with the creation of the United States Department of Labor. Along with the Pennsylvania Department of Labor and Industry, established the same year, Progressive Era reforms delineated the role of the federal and state governments in mediating and arbitrating disputes between capital and labor.

Though anthracite mineworkers secured some concessions in 1902 they could not weather the long-term decline of the industry for which they labored. The advent of alternative energy sources, continued labor-management strife, endemic union and industry corruption, company disinvestments, and other factors led to anthracite's decline. From the Great Depression to the 1959 Knox Mine Disaster it had become evident that anthracite would not recover. According to the Pennsylvania Department of Environmental Protection, one hundred years after the strike of 1902 the anthracite industry employed about one thousand workers who produced four million tons; an astonishing plunge from its peak of 180,000 workers in 1915 and the production record of one hundred million tons attained in 1917.

Anthracite's past is not at all dissimilar from Pennsylvania's other industrial stories. Like steel, coke, railroads, and textiles its history is replete with themes of immigration, industrialization, capital investment, technology, labor activism, regionalism, and economic transition. An argument can be made that, historically, there are few fundamental cultural, social, or economic differences between the experiences of locales such as Aliquippa, Johnstown, Steelton, or Easton with those of Scranton, Shenandoah, Coaldale, or Mahanoy City. Recognizing and interpreting these histories contributes to a broader understanding of the Pennsylvania—and the human—experience.

The proceedings in the pages that follow in part represent public commemoration of the Anthracite Coal Strike of 1902. In the fall of 1999 a planning committee was formed to observe and interpret the events of 1902 one hundred years later. With the support of the Pennsylvania Humanities Council, Pennsylvania Historical and Museum Commission, Pennsylvania Labor History Society, Luzerne County Historical Society, and Luzerne County Community College, the committee grew to include representatives from over twenty regional and statewide organizations who collaborated to bring about an extraordinary centennial commemoration. Events that took place from October 24 to 27, 2002, included a children's anthracite history program, state historical marker dedications in Scranton, Coaldale, and Shenandoah, the Pennsylvania Labor History Society's annual awards dinner held at St. Michael's Ukrainian Church in Shenandoah, a public history symposium held at Luzerne County Community College, and an exhibit opening at the Anthracite Heritage Museum in Scranton. The papers in these proceedings are those presented by a variety of scholars at Luzerne County Community College on October 26th. They examine numerous aspects of the "Great Strike."

In addition to acknowledging the relevance of the events of 1902, the commemoration remains, in itself, historic. The collaboration to bring it about transcended institutions, regions, and peoples so often ascribed to pockets of anthracite Pennsylvania and, indeed, the Commonwealth itself. In the pages of this book lies much of the history of the 1902 anthracite coal strike and how it is viewed one hundred years later. It is a history, not unlike so many others, that merits recollection and interpretation.

East Market Street, Looking Toward Public Square, Wilkes-Barre, PA. Real-photo postcard by Ambrose W. Zwiebel, circa 1902. Author's collection.

Beyond "The Great Coal Strike":
The Anthracite Region in 1902

Robert A. Janosov

Prelude: Celebrating the New Year

In Wilkes-Barre and Pottsville on Wednesday, January 1st, the weather was seasonal with the mercury registering around 20 degrees, although it seemed colder because of a "biting wind." It was much different from the unusually warm Christmas a week earlier and a disastrous flood that had caused "havoc" and millions of dollars in damage throughout the anthracite region in mid-December. Flooding continued when over three inches of heavy rain from Saturday, December 28, through Sunday, December 29, caused the Lehigh, Susquehanna, and Schuylkill rivers to swell over their banks, producing "great damage" in eastern Pennsylvania. The freak winter downpour left a "trail of disaster" in several southern states as well.[1]

Celebrations of the New Year in Pennsylvania's anthracite region ranged from raucous to elegant, and were seemingly unaffected by the flooding earlier in the week and the return of cold weather. In Wilkes-Barre, large numbers of the "younger element" filled the streets for most of the evening on December 31. They marched noisily throughout center city, arriving at the courthouse on Public Square just before midnight. As the hour approached midnight on the courthouse clock, the din of tin horns "augmented considerably by the shrill blowing of the colliery whistles and the ringing of bells made a rousing welcome."[2] Street demonstrations were a major feature of Pottsville's celebration as well. A masked carnival, organized by Pottsville's Elks Lodge, began at ten o'clock with hundreds parading in "grotesque costume." The parade featured numerous floats, representatives of the town's fire companies, military companies, and the Third Brigade Band. Each Elk carried a torch so the "line of march was a blaze of light." The noise kept "every serious resident in a state boarding on nervous prostration" until after midnight.[3]

More subdued gatherings, watch-night services, were sponsored by many of the region's Protestant denomination churches, providing time for quiet reflection and meditation. The region's social clubs hosted open houses and dances on both New Year's Eve and New Year's Day. Pottsville's Turtle Club held their annual New Year's dance at the Union Hall with Seltzer's orchestra providing music. Wilkes-Barre's élite Westmoreland Club held open house for members and guests from morning to midnight on New Year's Eve. The club provided an "elegant lunch," including claret Club House punch, oysters, and assorted side dishes. The West End Club's open house featured a "general feast." The Concordia Society had open house highlighting a string orchestra and an impromptu program of music by society members.[4]

The premier social event of the season in the region was the Annual Assembly,[5] which served the dual purpose of commemorating the New Year and providing a stage for the annual "coming out" of debutantes. The Pottsville Assembly Ball, held on December 30, 1901, in Union Hall, had been held every year since 1837. Music provided by Seltzer's orchestra kept the social élite of Pottsville and neighboring towns dancing until "a late hour."[6] However, the fleeting coverage of the event by the Pottsville newspaper is perhaps an indication of the declining status of an élite in the city by 1902. By the turn of the century most of Pottsville's major business was dominated by the Philadelphia and Reading Railroad Company.[7] Any "coming out" of debutantes from families somehow related to Pottsville through significant business interests probably occurred in Philadelphia.

Centre and Mahantongo Streets, Pottsville. Two-panel postcard circa 1902, published by George V. Miller & Co., Scranton. Author's collection.

Wilkes-Barre's 23rd Annual Assembly Ball provides a different impression. Held on New Year's Eve in the Ninth Regiment Armory on South Main Street, "the only space large enough to accommodate the throng," it was the "crowning social function of the year" attended by a firmly entrenched social élite of Wilkes-Barre's first families and economic leaders. The guest list included such names as Conyngham, Miner, Reynolds, Shoemaker, Bedford, Darling, Nesbitt, and Dorrance, just to name a few. Debutantes included: the Misses Sharpe, Miss Payne, Miss Butler, Miss Conyngham, and others. The armory was elaborately decorated with holly branches, evergreen tresses in pots, clusters of palms, and rubber plants at the entrance. The dancing room was separated from the entrance by a floral partition and colorful fabric streamers "hung from the various gallery points, radiating all to the centre chandelier of the ceiling." Describing the event as opulent, yet fashionable, the *Wilkes-Barre Record* concluded its commentary with an observation that "no such wealth of sartorial accomplishment is ever lavished on a social event as on this occasion."[8]

December's unusual weather allowed the editors of the *Wilkes-Barre Record* to wax eloquently in weather-related language to emphasize, "The prospects for the New Year upon which the world this morning enters are bright with promise. No threatening storm clouds portending industrial depression, financial panic or national distress of any kind, are visible on this dawning of the New Year." Continuing, the editors proclaimed: "The national skies are clear, and the sun of prosperity shines as brightly as at any time in the history of the republic." Finally, their forecast concluded that the country entered the New Year "without the slightest cause to fear disturbing agitations in matters relating to the nation's industries, its finance, or its general economic policies."[9] The *Pottsville Republican* echoed the *Record's* optimism by proclaiming "the new year opens with a higher degree of prosperity and of promise than any other previous year than can be found in any other country on the globe."[10] Events and the weather too would soon dispel this New Year's exuberance. Before Easter more devastating flooding would occur and by May the region would find itself embroiled in an epic labor struggle that would severely strain both regional and national resources.

Contextual Framework

The New Year was 1902 and most serious students of northeastern Pennsylvania's anthracite region associate it with "the Great Anthracite Coal Strike," an event of monumental consequence in American history.

The development of the anthracite industry during the nineteenth century played a vital role in the expansion of the American economy and helped "determine the timing and process of accelerated growth and institutional change in American manufacturing and mining."[11] By 1902, anthracite coal had become the major fuel source for domestic heating throughout the northeastern United States and was used extensively by America's railroads and in a wide range of manufacturing industries. Anthracite workers were organized into the nation's biggest union and were challenging its "most powerful industrial combination—a cartel of anthracite railroad operators and absentee "barons" in total control of an exclusive resource."[12] The strike's potential, as seen by a contemporary British economist, could have "such social consequences as the world has never seen."[13] So associating 1902 with the strike is appropriate because, according to labor historian Perry Blatz, it was one of "America's most significant labor disputes."[14] It was a bitter battle involving some 140,000 United Mine Workers led by their union president, John Mitchell; a group of particularly unsympathetic mine owners, whose spokesman, George C. Baer, outraged almost everyone in the country with his so-called "divine right" letter; the trust-busting president of the United States, Theodore Roosevelt; the Wall Street financier and the era's epitome of capitalism, John Pierpont Morgan; and a host of other significant players. Ultimately, the strike was settled with no clear winners or losers, but the settlement was "most important for the labor movement in the United States" because the "federal government had intervened in a labor dispute for the first time in the country's history, not to break a strike, but to bring about a peaceful settlement."[15]

Certainly, from a labor history perspective, 1902 was the "year of the great strike." But it is also a year that fits into a variety of other historical perspectives as well.

1902 comes at the early end of the Progressive Era (1900–1917), a period in American history when reformers sought to use the government as an agency of human welfare. Progressive reformers crusaded against abuses in urban politics and corporate robber barons. They promoted fair labor practices, child welfare, conservation, and consumer protection. They challenged America's tradition of isolationism, believing the country had a moral obligation to spread democracy and an economic opportunity to reap profits in foreign markets.[16] It was a movement, as defined by Richard Hofstadter, that attempted "to develop the moral will, the intellectual insight, and the political and administrative agencies to remedy the accumulated evils and negligences of a period of industrial growth."[17]

1902 was also part of the "Pre-World War I Era" (1871–1914), a period when European nations engaged in "intense rivalry, aggravated by diplomatic realignments, military rearmament, and colonial competition" with an "isolated" America beginning to join the mix. Over forty years of growing tensions eventually led to open conflict when "modern and modernizing societies, armed with modern weapons, recklessly entered a modern war" with unparalleled slaughter.[18]

Yet, the twenty-four years (1890–1914) before the catastrophe of World War I have been portrayed *la belle époque* (the beautiful time) by many as well. It was a period when "pleasure reigned" and *joie de vivre* characterized everyday life, especially in Paris, but was also exemplified in the United States in general and more specifically in the anthracite region of Pennsylvania. The pursuits of pleasure and of leisure, an "atmosphere of gaieté, recreation, frivolity," were very much a part of 1902, albeit only for those who could afford them.[19]

"The Edwardian Era" (1901–1919) is another historical characterization relating especially to the wealthy that encompasses 1902. The era corresponds with the reign of King Edward VII of England (1901–1910), but featured a European and American "style" that transcended the king's reign. Both Europeans and Americans, who "indulged in cuisine, fashion, entertainment, and travel as never before," experienced the first rewards of modern

Sixth Street, Shamokin, postcard circa 1902. Author's collection

industrialization and mass-produced abundance. In the arts, the era produced Post-Impressionism, Expressionism, Cubism, and, most popular in mainstream America and Europe, Art Nouveau, which affected the design of architecture, clothing (particularly the emergence of curvaceous styles for women, symbolized by the "Harrison Fisher Woman" and the "Gibson Girl" in popular American magazines and books), furniture, jewelry, household articles, and commercial art.[20]

Despite its regional and national significance, the Anthracite Coal Strike is not the focus of this essay, nor are any of the above-mentioned movements, eras, styles, or any other specific conceptual frameworks created by historians. The strike has been chronicled by scores of historians previously and will be analyzed carefully from a variety of perspectives by eminent historians in the remaining pages of this volume.

This essay attempts to provide a context for the strike by surveying the kaleidoscope of people, events, and some of the realities of life existing during 1902 in the anthracite region of Pennsylvania. For, while the Anthracite Coal Strike was a distinctly noteworthy feature of 1902, life went on, people encountered a wide range of experiences that affected their lives. Some suffered from the excesses of unbridled capitalism, while other enjoyed its fruits. Some children went to school, while others labored in mills and mines. Some ate blue point oysters, while others ate kielbasa or halusky. Some drank hard liquor, while others crusaded against the evils of "booze." Some women enjoyed newfound leisure time, while others toiled long hours in garment or silk factories. Some traveled to newly developed resorts in the Pocono Mountains to enjoy a vacation from work; others rode trolleys to amusement parks. Certainly from a labor history perspective 1902 was the "year of the great strike." But it is also a year when a variety of other social, economic, cultural, political, and demographic realities existed, many of which reflect broader national and even international trends. This essay, then, should be viewed as an incomplete portrait, a few brush strokes, chosen somewhat haphazardly by the author, to portray the broad spectrum of life in the anthracite region during 1902.

The Setting

Much of northeastern Pennsylvania is popularly designated as the "anthracite region" since it contains the largest concentration of anthracite coal deposits in the world. Yet, its fame preceded the large-scale extraction of coal. During the eighteenth and early nineteenth centuries the region was hailed as one of rugged but great beauty. It was considered "wild" and "forbidding"; nevertheless, part of the region, the Wyoming Valley, was described as "the best, and the pleasantest land we ever saw" by early settlers. The region was memorialized in literature and art and was known throughout the English-speaking world for its aesthetic beauty.[21] Engravings like Jacob Cist's *Upper and Lower Falls of Solomon's Creek* that appeared in *The Portfolio* in 1809 record natural features of the anthracite region's Wyoming Valley, but also suggest early nineteenth-century views "of the sublime, the beautiful, and the picturesque." The region's beauty and the "harmony of the human and the natural world" it displayed was caught for the world by William Henry Bartlett's drawings and watercolors, transformed into engravings for *American Scenery* (1840), a picturesque travel book published in England, New York, and various foreign language editions. Thomas Cole, Thomas Doughty, Jasper Francis Cropsey, some of the leading lights of the Hudson River school, painted the Susquehanna River and its tributaries flowing through the anthracite region. Doughty painted numerous views of the Schuylkill and Delaware rivers as well. "Forest Scene on the Lehigh" and "Forest Scene on the Tobihanna, Alleghany Mountains" drawn by Karl Bodmer and "Falls on the Lackawanna Near Tunkhannock, Pa" a lithograph drawn by E. Whitefield, are other examples of nineteenth-century landscapes focusing on the impressive landscape of the anthracite region.[22]

By 1902 much of the pristine beauty, the virgin forests, and the clear mountain streams filled with fish of Pennsylvania's anthracite region had vanished, leading Peter Roberts in his sociological portrait of the region, *Anthracite Coal Communities*, to describe the physical environment as "unclean," filled with a "rancid stench," with streams of "foul water laden with coal dust" turning into a "mass of black flowing stuff that is a curse to all forms of organic life,"[23] the legacy of the anthracite industry. Virgin forests, beautiful valleys, and clear mountain streams had been replaced by culm (coal waste) heaps and scores of coal breakers dominating the region's skyline.

Anthracite coal deposits spread over 484 square miles of northeastern Pennsylvania in four distinct, "canoe-shaped" fields, the Northern Field, the Eastern Middle Field, the Western Middle Field, and the Southern Field. The deposits are found in the nine counties of Wayne, Susquehanna, Lackawanna, Luzerne, Carbon, Schuylkill, Columbia, Northumberland, and Dauphin.[24] Most of the coal lies in the five counties of Carbon, Lackawanna, Luzerne, Northumberland, and Schuylkill. The territory is bounded on the north and west by the Susquehanna River and its tributaries and on the east by the Lehigh River. The southern boundary is defined by the Blue Mountains, part of the Appalachian chain. Both the Lehigh and Schuylkill rivers flow into the Delaware River to the east, and the Susquehanna flows southwesterly to the Chesapeake Bay. At the turn of the century, Scranton (102,026) and Wilkes-Barre (51,721) were the principal cities of the Northern Field, and were the region's largest cities. Hazleton (14,230) was the dominant city of the Eastern Middle Field, while Shenandoah (20,321) and Shamokin (18,202) were foremost in the Western Middle Field. Pottsville (15,710), Lansford (4,888), Tamaqua (7,267), and Mauch Chunk (4,029) were the principal cities of the Southern Field.

Demographic Growth

By the turn of the century, as the anthracite industry expanded, the five primary anthracite counties experienced substantial population growth, concentrated for the most part in large urban centers and numerous mining villages. This growth was part of the national trend toward urbanization begun in the late nineteenth century. During the period 1900–1920 the urban population of the United States, in places with populations of 2,500 or more, increased by 80%. Eight out of ten new immigrants to the United States settled in cities. Most of the urban growth was concentrated in the northern states of New York, Pennsylvania, Massachusetts, Illinois, and Ohio, where over half of the entire urban population lived in 1890. In 1900 six out of ten people in the North Atlantic States and three out of ten in the Midwest lived in cities. The phenomenon affected the growth of large cities to the greatest extent, but small towns and villages grew in population as well. From 1880 to 1920 the number of villages and towns from less than a thousand to up to 10,000 nearly doubled. By 1900 almost 55% of Pennsylvania's population was urban.[25]

Between 1890 and 1900 the population of the five major anthracite counties rose 24%, from 610,776 to 759,300. (CHART 1) Population in the two most populous counties, Lackawanna and Luzerne, rose 36% and 28% respectively. Scranton in Lackawanna County and Wilkes-Barre in Luzerne County experienced 36% and 37% growth. In fact, Scranton and Wilkes-Barre accounted for 20% of the total population of the five anthracite counties. By 1900 Scranton was the third-largest city in Pennsylvania, and the 38th-largest

CHART 1
ANTHRACITE COUNTIES
POPULATION CHANGE 1890–1900

COUNTY	1890	1900
CARBON	38,624	44,510
LACKAWANNA	142,088	193,831
LUZERNE	201,203	257,121
NORTHUMBERLAND	74,698	90,911
SCHUYLKILL	154,163	172,927
TOTAL	610,776	759,300

city in the nation.[26] Wilkes-Barre was the 75th largest. Plymouth borough in Luzerne County saw the greatest percentage (47%) increase in population, while Pottsville in Schuylkill County experienced only an 11% increase, signaling the end of Pottsville's "boom-town" growth of the nineteenth century. Sixteen municipalities with population of 4,000 or more in the five counties included 40% (304,030) of the five-county total population.[27] (CHART 2)

Immigration from Europe accounts for most of this population growth. European immigrants had been arriving in northeastern Pennsylvania in a steady stream for about one hundred years. Most came from the British Isles or Germany. After 1880, the character and scale of this migration changed, and thousands of southern and eastern Europeans arrived in northeastern Pennsylvania to take advantage of job opportunities associated with the expanding anthracite coal industry. In the five major anthracite counties, 26% of the population was foreign-born by 1890. The combined total of foreign-born and those who were native-born of foreign parents amounted to 46% of the population. By 1900 the percentage of foreign-born declined to 24%, but the combined total of foreign-born and their children born in the United States rose to 58%. (See CHART 3 & CHART 4) By 1900 around half of the mine employees in the region were "non-English speaking."[28] The reality of such a dramatic change in the composition of the population in a relatively short period caused significant social, cultural, and economic tension in the region. Often referred to as "foreigners" or by more specific national designations such as "polander" or "Pittston Italian" in area newspapers, the new immigrant residents of the region were viewed as socially inferior and dangerous by the native (Anglo-Saxon) population. Commenting on a murder committed by two "foreign" miners, the *Wilkes-Barre Record* included the following judgment about "foreigners," which was typical of the era:

CHART 2
ANTHRACITE MUNICIPALITIES
POPULATION CHANGE 1890–1900

MUNICIPALITY	1890	1900
Scranton	75,215	102,026
Wilkes-Barre	37,718	51,721
Shenandoah	15,944	20,321
Shamokin	14,403	18,202
Pottsville	14,117	15,710
Hazleton	11,872	14,230
Plymouth	9,344	13,694
Carbondale	10,833	13,538
Pittston	10,302	12,556
Nanticoke	10,044	12,116
Tamaqua	6,054	7,267
Lansford	4,004	4,888
Minersville	3.504	4,815
St. Clair	3,680	4,638
Forest City	2,319	4,279
Mauch Chunk	4,101	4,029
TOTAL	233,454	304,030

The non-English speaking people of certain classes in the anthracite coal regions are making a shocking record. They use the knife, the pistol, the bludgeon, or any other deadly weapon, with a recklessness that is absolutely shocking to other classes of people.... These people by the lawlessness and crime, impose a frightful burden upon the taxpayers and also give the county a notoriety for crime which it would not deserve but for these foreign outlaws.[29]

One institution particularly affected by the tide of immigration was the region's Roman Catholic Church, founded and dominated by Irish Catholics. The Scranton Diocese, formed in 1868, encompassed eleven counties, including the two most-populous anthracite counties, Lackawanna and

Luzerne. Since most of the new immigrant residents of the region were Roman Catholic, the number of Catholics in the diocese rose dramatically. By 1890 the number of Catholics grew to 165,239 and reached 223,010 by 1900, 29% of the total population within the area of the Diocese of Scranton. Since most of the new immigrants were eastern and southern Europeans, who brought with them different languages, customs, and religious traditions, the diocese was confronted everywhere with demands for "national" parishes. By 1900 the number of parishes in the diocese rose to one hundred, most of which were "national," serving the diverse nationalities that now dominated. Examples include: Wilkes-Barre's Blessed Virgin (Polish) parish on Park Avenue and Ecclesia Slavica (Slovak) on North Main Street, Hazleton's St. Joseph (Slovak) parish on Laurel Street, Nanticoke's Holy Trinity (Polish) on Hanover Street, St. Casimir's (Lithuanian) in Pittston, and St. Mary's (Italian) in Old Forge.[30]

"Diamond City" and "Electric City": Wilkes-Barre and Scranton as Analogous Urban Centers

As population in the anthracite region grew and was concentrated in urban areas, Wilkes-Barre and Scranton quickly became not only the largest cities in northeastern Pennsylvania in 1902, but they were the principal political, economic, social, and cultural centers of the region as well. The "Diamond City" designation for Wilkes-Barre is credited to Oscar Jewell Harvey, Luzerne County's turn-of-the-century patrician historian. Harvey's characterization is based on the city's diamond-shaped Public Square, "underlaid with a vast wealth of black diamonds, and overlaid with hospitality, cultivation and beauty – qualities which, like the chief characteristics of the diamond, are distinctive and attractive."[31] Since Scranton had the first electric-car street railway system (1886) in Pennsylvania and the United States, it was christened the "Electric City."[32] While Hazleton and Pottsville served in similar roles for the Middle and Southern Anthracite Fields, neither compares in scope of power and influence to Wilkes-Barre and Scranton. In fact, both Shenandoah and Shamokin were larger than Pottsville in 1902, which was the largest and most dominant community in the southern coalfield in the first half of the nineteenth century, and the overwhelmingly dominant influence in the region emanated from Philadelphia and the corporate power of the Philadelphia and Reading Railroad.[33]

Wilkes-Barre is the oldest town in Northeastern Pennsylvania and became the county seat of Luzerne County in 1786. Designated a borough in 1806, it was incorporated as a city in 1871. According to official census figures, Wilkes-Barre was approximately half the size of Scranton in 1900. However, the census figures are somewhat deceiving when a comparison is made of the physical size of both cities. Wilkes-Barre included 4.85 square

miles, while Scranton encompassed 18.5 square miles, secured through an-
nexation of contiguous communities. In 1906, the Wilkes-Barre Board of
Trade conducted an analysis, based on the 1900 census, of the city's population potential if independent boroughs and townships contiguous to the city
in a three-mile radius of Public Square, an area comparable in size to
Scranton, were annexed. The result was a "Greater Wilkes-Barre" with a
population of 104,762, almost 3,000 persons larger than Scranton.[34] (The
author, raised and educated in Wilkes-Barre, requests tolerance for some
chauvinism here, even though the figures are correct!)

*North River Street, Wilkes-Barre. Real-photo postcard by A.A.
Zwiebel, circa 1902. Author's collection.*

Despite a business depression caused by the anthracite coal strike,
Wilkes-Barre was not affected as badly as other towns in the region that were
almost exclusively dependent on coal. Wilkes-Barre in 1902 was a city showing signs of progressive growth, diversifying its economic base and consoli-
dating its position as one of the region's dominant urban centers. The assessed value of Wilkes-Barre property was over thirty-four million dollars,
representing one-third of the total valuation of Luzerne County. Six major
railroads connected Wilkes-Barre to the large urban centers on the east
coast, northern New York, the Great Lakes, and Canada, providing transportation for the various commodities produced in the city as well as the
most valuable asset—coal.[35] While coal production in 1902 was down considerably because of the strike, to 41,340,935 tons, the previous year had
been the best ever achieved by the industry, with a production of over
67,000,000 tons. More than twenty-four thousand employees with average
annual earnings of $377.76 mined over 50% of the coal in the Wyoming re-
gion, which included the Wilkes-Barre area.[36] The nine Wilkes-Barre banks

displayed another measure of the wealth of the community, with over two million dollars in capital, almost three million surplus dollars, and twelve and a half million dollars in deposits.

The Wilkes-Barre Lace Manufacturing Company. Postcard circa 1902. Author's collection.

Ninety-six incorporated companies operating within the city bolstered Wilkes-Barre's economy. These included the Hazard Wire Rope Company, the largest of its type in the state, and the Sheldon Axel Works, the largest in the country. Vulcan Iron Works at the intersection of South Main and Blackman streets produced locomotives and mine machinery. Wilkes-Barre Lace Manufacturing Company on Courtright Street in the city's north end was one of the largest manufacturers of Nottingham lace in the country. Two major silk mills operated in the city, Bamford Brothers on South Empire Street and Hess, Goldsmith and Company, which had plants on Blackman Street and Waller Street. Mills such as these and others that operated throughout the county primarily employed women earning an average of $194.90 annually, while men employed in the county's 1,290 manufacturing establishments earned approximately $492 a year. Wilkes-Barre and Luzerne County manufacturing firms also employed over seven hundred salaried officials and clerks, who earned an average of $1005.00 annually. The county's salaried officials and clerks, combined with nearly fourteen hundred proprietors, formed a rapidly expanding professional class, many of whom lived in Wilkes-Barre.[37]

The residents included in *The Scranton and Wilkes-Barre Society Blue Book* are one measure of the size of Wilkes-Barre's more affluent and socially prestigious population. Qualification for membership in the city's "social register" included affiliation with one or more of the city's élite social clubs, including the Westmoreland Club, the Wyoming Valley Country Club, the D.A.R. Wyoming Valley Chapter, the New Century Club, the West End Wheelmen, the Concordia Society, the Malt Club, and the Commercial Club. The Blue Book listed over fourteen hundred individuals in 1900 that lived in grand residences primarily on South River and South Franklin streets, although the one-block Mallery Place, off West River Street, contained twenty-seven listings, making it one of the most impressive (though perhaps transitional for some) addresses in the city. One family residing on Mallery Place in 1902 was that of Mr. And Mrs. Frederick J. Weckesser. Weckesser was a top executive of Wilkes-Barre's F.M. Kirby and Company, the five-and-dime chain. He arrived in Wilkes-Barre in 1899 and served as general manager and buyer for the Kirby chain until 1912. He helped engineer the merger of the Kirby and Woolworth companies and was made a member of the board of directors of F.W. Woolworth Company. His promotion apparently required a more substantial residence, so he commissioned the New York society architect C.H.P. Gilbert to design a new "house" on South Franklin Street. The result was a French *Chateauesque* mansion, which today serves as the administration building for Wilkes University.[38]

The Stegmaier Brewing Company produced 111,860 barrels of beer in 1901, making it the largest brewery business in Pennsylvania outside of Philadelphia and Pittsburgh. Stegmaier responded to a changing market trend, greater demand for bottled beer, by erecting a bottling house across Market Street from the main brewery in 1902. The bottling house, designed by the Wilkes-Barre architectural firm of McCormick and French, was a three-story rectangular, brick -and-stone building with similar exterior decoration as the other brewery buildings. Since federal law banned bottling on the brewery premises, a tunnel containing beer pipelines was constructed under Market Street connecting the brewery with the bottling house.[39] The total output of beer by Luzerne County's breweries during 1901 was 326,616 barrels, causing the *Wilkes-Barre Record* to produce an interesting calculation in March 1902. The paper pointed out that total production in 1901 equated to 1,306,464 quarter kegs of beer, "sufficient to allow five kegs to every man, woman, and child in the county," despite the refusal by the Luzerne County Court to renew some one hundred and eleven liquor licenses. The action by the court, according to the *Wilkes-Barre Record*, demonstrated that the judges believed there were "enough thirst extinguishing factories to satisfy the demands of the people of Luzerne County." The license refusals were credited as a "decided victory" for the Anti-Saloon League, which had gathered evidence against most of the saloons and hotels denied licenses.[40]

Harry Hillman's Academy, Wilkes-Barre. German-made postcard circa 1902. Author's collection.

The city boasted twenty-seven miles of paved streets after considerable paving work was completed during the year. The Wilkes-Barre school system included nineteen elementary schools and one high school with about eight thousand children attending on a regular basis. Salaries for male teachers ranged from $600 to $1800, while female teachers averaged from $360 to $800. In addition to the public schools, two private academies, Harry Hillman Academy for boys and the Wilkes-Barre Institute for girls, operated in the city along with five Catholic parochial schools (St. Ann's Academy, St. Mary's Academy, St. Mary's Elementary School, St. Mary's Polish Catholic School, and St. Nicholas Parochial School). Wilkes-Barre Business College & School of Shorthand, Wilkes-Barre College of Music, the Atlantic School of Osteopathy, and a branch of Scranton's International Correspondence School enrolled students as well.[41]

The city's electric trolley car system operated by the Wilkes-Barre, Dallas and Harvey's Lake Railroad and the Wilkes-Barre and Wyoming Valley Traction Company reached every city and town within ten miles. The Harvey's Lake Line, purchased by the Lehigh Valley Railroad, began to run passenger service to the lake in 1887, providing inexpensive transportation for thousands of Wilkes-Barre's working- and middle-class residents. According to lake historian F. Charles Petrillo, the advent of the trolley system ushered in the "Golden Years" at Harvey's Lake, making the lake "one of the state's most fashionable resorts."[42]

Another summertime option made available by the Wilkes-Barre and Wyoming Valley Traction Company was Hanover Park (in later years known as Sans Souci Park) located in Hanover Township adjacent to Wilkes-Barre. A short trolley ride brought thousands to the park to enjoy the amusement rides, a live show at the park's summer theatre, or special events. On Independence Day, a baseball game matched the best team from Lackawanna County, the Sunsets, with the top-ranked team from Luzerne County, the Hanover Nine. Hanover won. Fireworks provided constant noise, but police confiscated numerous .38 caliber pistols from young boys, preventing serious injuries. Labor Day, celebrated in the midst of the coal strike, attracted thousands to a parade and demonstration in Wilkes-Barre followed by a massive picnic at the park.[43] Despite the tensions created by the long strike, one can imagine many young miners humming the tune of the year's most popular song, "In the Good Old Summer Time," dreaming of the day

> When your day's work is over then you are in clover,
> And life is one beautiful rhyme,
> No trouble annoying, each one enjoying
> The good old summertime[44]

While the city's middle and working classes enjoyed the pleasures of Harvey's Lake and Hanover Park, the city's more affluent residents traveled by train to their "cottages" in Glen Summit Springs near Wilkes-Barre, although a severe fire in April endangered the élite "mountain resort" causing "no little excitement among the summer residents."[45] Presumably, many of the more affluent city residents also traveled to one of the many flourishing Pocono Mountain resorts located nearby. Resorts like the Montanesca, the Churleigh Hotel, the Kittatinny, and others were marketed primarily to residents of New York and Philadelphia by the Monroe County Mountain Resort Association and the Lackawanna Railroad, but drew tourists from northeastern Pennsylvania as well. Demand was so great in 1902 that resorts turned twenty thousand tourists away.[46]

For those who were disappointed and those who could not afford to travel, Wilkes-Barre offered a great variety of entertainment. In May the Forepaugh & Sells Brothers' circus arrived in town, attracting a "mass of humanity" in downtown Wilkes-Barre by eight o'clock in the morning to watch the traditional circus parade. The *Wilkes-Barre Record* speculated the large number of people in attendance was due to the coal strike, since "the only people who worked being those engaged about the manufacturing industries."[47] Wilkes-Barre's theatres, the Nesbitt and the Grand Opera House, offered an endless variety of plays, musical programs, lectures, and moving pictures created by Wilkes-Barre's own Lyman Howe.[48] Baseball offered another diversion. In and around Wilkes-Barre numerous teams participated in the "anthracite leagues" with games played mostly on Sundays. The Wilkes-Barre Baseball Club, organized in 1885 and nicknamed the "Coal Barons," played their games in West

Side Park, across the river from the city with a local boy and future hall-of-famer, Ed Walsh, pitching during the 1902 season.[49]

Wilkes-Barre's commercial enterprises thrived in 1902, despite the coal strike. Flower, Dick, & Walker (The Boston Store), Lazarus Brothers, Isaac Long's, Simon Long's, the Jonas Long's & Sons, the Bee Hive, the Globe Store, large drygoods stores, precursors to the more modern department store, offered a wide range of goods to their clientele. The stores featured large plate-glass windows for "window shopping," an increasingly popular pastime for consumers. The new Globe Store building on Public Square featured "large staircases and elevators" and "large waiting rooms and lavatories," was lighted by gas and electricity, and "furnished with the most improved cash carrier system."[50] Twenty-one hotels graced the downtown, the largest being the Sterling on West Market Street, the Redington on East Market Street, and the Wyoming Valley on South River Street. Eighteen jewelry stores, three Chinese laundries, at least ten furniture stores, three oyster dealers, restaurants, milliners, clothiers, cigar and tobacco stores, and one hundred forty-four licensed liquor dealers serviced Wilkes-Barre's expanding population.

View of Pittston. Postcard circa 1902. Author's collection.

While prosperity seemed the order of the day, Wilkes-Barre and surrounding towns did suffer a series of calamities during the year. A smallpox epidemic raged from the spring of 1901 through May 1902. Two hundred and one cases were recorded in Luzerne County, with forty-eight deaths attributed to the disease. Fear of the disease caused Wilkes-Barre to establish a quarantine against all towns on the west side of the Susquehanna and Pittston. The city's sanitary committee employed clerks and issued passes into the city only to those showing certificates of vaccination. During January a scarlet fever epidemic struck Wilkes-Barre's Rolling Mill Hill and Heights sections. Almost one hundred cases and two deaths were reported. Another devastating flood, causing the greatest damage by water until that time in the history of the Wyoming Valley, occurred on March 1 and 2, when the Susquehanna River reached 31.3 feet at Wilkes-Barre. Hundreds of houses were destroyed, seven people lost their lives, all of the streets in the city below South Street were flooded, and all of South River Street was under water. The flood was followed on March 5 by fifteen inches of snow, complicating clean-up efforts.[51] A major delay in the construction of a new county courthouse occurred when controversy arose first over the transfer of land for the building, and then over the awarding of architectural and building contracts. The courthouse was not completed until 1909. Labor unrest, in addition to the coal strike, caused considerable problems in Wilkes-Barre and surrounding towns during the year as well. Employees at the West End Knitting Mill in Plymouth struck in January. In March workers at Wilkes-Barre Lace Manufacturing struck in support of two boys discharged for violating rules. Painters in Wilkes-Barre struck in April, another strike occurred at Wilkes-Barre Lace in June, and in December carpenters declared a strike while working on a new federal government building on South Main Street.[52]

Scranton emerged as an urban center later than Wilkes-Barre, but by 1902 it was a city both physically and demographically larger. Settlers from Connecticut and New York moved into the area around what would eventually become Scranton and Lackawanna County in the 1760s. They created farming communities, including Providence, Slocum Hollow, and Old Forge, and rudimentary industries along the Lackawanna River. The age of anthracite in the area began when the Wurtz brothers mined coal in Carbondale and that city seemed destined to become the region's industrial center.[53] The forces that shaped the development of Scranton as an urban center began in the last half of the nineteenth century with the growth of the anthracite iron and coal industries. Scranton's Lackawanna Iron Works, founded in the 1840s, became one of the largest producers of T rail for America's rapidly expanding railroads. As Lackawanna grew and more employees were hired, the company hired Joel Amsden, an architect, to lay out the plan for the city of Scranton in 1850–51. By 1852, more than 3,000 people lived in the immediate vicinity around the Lackawanna iron furnaces. This development reflected a shift from a predominantly rural industry to one that would become increasingly urbanized as the size of individual plants and the need for workers expanded dramatically. The growth of the iron industry required better transportation links to markets in New York and Philadelphia, resulting in the formation of the Delaware, Lackawanna, & Western Railroad in 1852, which also led to widespread mining of anthracite in the Lackawanna Valley.[54] The combined impetuses of anthracite iron and coal caused the city of Scranton to grow rapidly as immigrants were drawn to the region by employment opportunities in the iron, coal, and railroad industries. By the 1860s, through the efforts of local businessmen and politicians, the state legislature voted to incorporate the neighboring boroughs of Hyde Park and Providence into Scranton, creating a municipal boundary that would permit future growth. However, Wilkes-Barre remained the county seat of a Luzerne County that included Scranton and all of the land comprising present-day Lackawanna County. In 1878, leaders in and around Scranton finally secured the formation of Lackawanna County and Scranton became the government and economic center of the Lackawanna Valley.[55]

Court House Square from Spruce Street, Scranton. German-made postcard circa 1902. Author's collection.

By the 1870s, Scranton boasted an ethnically diverse population of 20,000 residents. By 1880, the city had over 45,000 people and was the largest city in northeastern Pennsylvania. The city's population more than doubled to 102,026 by 1900. If the populations of both the "urban fringe" and "outer fringe" communities either adjacent to or near Scranton are taken into consideration, the 1900 population of metropolitan Scranton was 186,320.[56]

If Wilkes-Barre was able to withstand the depression associated with the anthracite coal strike as a result of its diversification, Scranton was in an even better position. From the late nineteenth century on, Scranton had placed much greater emphasis on diversification than Wilkes-Barre, so it had a higher percentage of workers employed in manufacturing. Moreover, Scranton had weathered a major economic catastrophe in 1901 when its oldest and largest firm, Lackawanna Iron and Steel, left the city for Buffalo, New York. Despite such a great loss, the assessed value of real estate in Scranton remained over sixty-five million dollars. Nearly twenty million dollars of capital was invested in the city's over seven hundred manufacturing and mechanical industries. Scranton's remaining industries, like the Dickson Manufacturing Company and the Scranton Stove Company that operated in the city since the 1850s, or the International Textbook Company, the Scranton Electric Construction Company, the Sauquoit Silk Manufacturing Company, the Scranton Button Manufacturing Company, the Scranton Lace Company, and the International Salt Company that emerged in the last decades of the nineteenth century, managed to employ over twelve thousand workers with combined payrolls over five million dollars. County-wide, another three hundred industries operated, making the total over one thousand manufacturing establishments operated by an equal number of proprietors. The total wages paid by these industries was over six million dollars, producing an average annual wage of four hundred dollars.[57]

The city had over seven hundred proprietors and more than six hundred salaried officials and clerks earning an average of $1,198.00 annually who, combined with the industrial proprietors, formed an affluent professional class, many of whom lived in Scranton's more fashionable neighborhoods, like those on Washington Avenue, Clay Avenue, Madison Avenue, the Hill section, or Green Ridge. Scranton's "social register" was larger than Wilkes-Barre's, numbering almost two thousand individuals affiliated with the city's prestigious social organizations, including the Scranton City Club, the Scranton Bicycle Club, the Scranton Country Club, the Physicians' Club, the Green Ridge Woman's Club, and the Scranton Engineering Club.[58]

On the opposite end of the socioeconomic spectrum were the extraordinarily large numbers of relatively recent immigrants who comprised a large portion of Scranton's and Lackawanna County's population. Twenty-eight percent of Scranton's population was foreign-born, nearly matching Lackawanna County's twenty-nine percent. In both the city and the county most were from southeastern European countries, followed by Irish and Germans respectively. County-wide the combination of foreign-born and their children born in the United States represented forty-two percent of the population. Most of these newcomers lived in well-defined neighborhoods in the city or in one of the many small towns surrounding Scranton. One or two ethnic groups often dominated Lackawanna Valley towns or the city's residential neighborhoods. Jessup and Old Forge were Italian. Simpson was Russian and Slovak. Minooka was Irish. Jermyn was Ruthenian and Russian. South Scranton was Polish.[59]

The combination of socioeconomic stratification and ethnic differences often led to disputes among the groups, or to discrimination. An 1896 dispute between Polish Catholics in South Scranton's Sacred Hearts parish led to the creation of the Polish National Catholic Church. By the summer of 1902, Father Francis Hodur, the clerical leader of the schism, announced support for the movement included ten congregations, eight priests, and 10,000 followers.[60]

One noteworthy example of discrimination involved Scranton's pride and joy—its electric streetcar system. In 1902, Scranton had over thirty-two miles of street railway. Put into service in 1886, the system earned the city the nickname "Electric City." Operated by the Scranton Railway Company, the system carried thousands of passengers both in Scranton proper and from the numerous communities throughout the county, despite a six-month streetcar workers strike that began in October 1901 and ended in April 1902.[61] Thousands of urban dwellers from the small mining towns in Lacka-wanna County that offered a measure of self-sufficiency relied on Scranton as a commercial, recreational, and cultural center. Scranton's rapidly ex-panding professional class often sought to distance itself from those stereo-typed as "the great unwashed." The railway company subtly discriminated against its working-class, ethnic patrons through the routing of some lines in order to protect its more affluent passengers. Of the thirty lines operated, most ran through the downtown business district except the Green Ridge Suburban, the Dunmore Suburban, Nay Aug Park, Providence, and the Green Ridge Peoples. Those lines were kept separate so "miners would not soil the seats used by residents of the wealthy neighborhoods" and ears would not be "assailed by the Babel of foreign tongues."[62]

Lincoln Lake in Nay Aug Park, Scranton. Postcard circa 1902.
Author's collection.

Scranton featured almost 150 miles of streets, with 21 miles paved. City leaders boasted of over 700 electric arc lights and roughly 100 acres of public parks. The city school system included 39 elementary schools and one high school. Eleven banks and nineteen railroad companies operated within the city limits. The city's literate population supported 28 newspapers and seven libraries. Four general hospitals administered to the health needs of the residents. The community's charitable spirit was demonstrated by support for the Florence Crittenden Mission, Saint Joseph's Foundling Home, and the Home for Friendless Women and Children.

Scrantonians worshiped in 92 churches and four synagogues. Scranton was the location of the executive offices of the Roman Catholic Diocese of Scranton, under the leadership of Bishop Michael J. Hoban. The diocesan offices administered to the needs of almost a quarter of a million Catholics living in the diocese and the approximately 12,000 children who attended Catholic parochial school in 1902.[63] Saint Thomas College on Wyoming Avenue, the first institution of higher learning founded in northeastern Pennsylvania, struggled through another year of low enrollments with a quasi-collegiate curriculum. Since the college was not yet officially chartered, diplomas were actually awarded by Saint John's College in Washington, D.C.[64]

Scranton had its share of calamities, along with a considerable amount of murder, "slashings," "beatings," robberies and gruesome suicides, during 1902, despite the general atmosphere of growth and prosperity. A smallpox epidemic ravaged the city and outlying towns through the whole year, forcing the vaccination of three thousand students. In February rabies afflicted the city as well. The "biggest flood in the history of Scranton" until that time hit the city on February 28. Railroad and street traffic was stopped, houses were inundated, and three bridges were swept away, while two boys drowned. Flsoodwaters were followed by a twelve-inch snowstorm on March 2. March also saw the house of one of Scranton's earliest settlers, Ira Tripp, burn to the ground. In addition to the coal strike and the streetcar strike, Scranton endured a tailors strike, a stove workers strike, and a carpenters strike.[65]

Despite natural disasters, epidemic disease, and "the great coal strike," Scrantonians were able to enjoy themselves. A new Scranton professional baseball team provided thrills during the spring and summer, but by the fall it failed. Yet, many city residents presumably followed the fortunes of Christy Mathewson, Factoryville native and future hall of famer, as he slumped with a 14-17 record with the New York Giants in 1902.[66] Scrantonians cheered a George Meier, who arrived in the city after a 13,000-mile bicycle ride. They listened to the great Polish pianist, Ignacy Jan Paderewski, at the 13th Regiment Armory. Lecturers William Jennings Bryan and Secretary of the Navy William Moody drew large crowds at Scranton's Lyceum. Even Scranton's newsboys were entertained with a picnic in Nay Aug Park in July and a Christmas dinner in December. The year ended with the premier social event of the year, the Annual Ball of Bachelors, held in the 13th Regiment Armory.[67]

The Scranton Times published two articles toward the end of the year that seem to foretell the future for Scranton, Wilkes-Barre, and the whole anthracite region. In an article on November 24, the newspaper reported that the Scranton police had been ordered to enforce a new ordinance limiting automobile speed in the city. Perhaps the article is an early signal of the "Age of the Automobile" in northeastern Pennsylvania and across the nation. While the automobile emerged in the United States a rich man's toy, by 1916 a Ford Model T sold for $360. In that year, U.S. manufacturers produced over 1.7 million cars and 181,348 commercial vehicles, Pennsylvania had over 230,000 motor vehicles registered, and Scranton's Board of Trade reported "3,000 pleasure cars and 1,000 motor trucks" in the city and its vicinity. By 1926, Pennsylvania had over 1.2 million motor vehicles registered, the third-highest total in the nation. The state claimed over 12,000 miles of highway, over 8,000 miles of which was paved, while Scranton had over 87 miles of paved streets. In Scranton's 1926 Annual Report of Public Works Department, the department director reported: "As traffic of today consists mostly of fast motor driven vehicles, cleaning and paving [streets] becomes a problem."[68] So the 1902 *Scranton Times* article signals Scranton's, the anthracite region's, and the nation's development as one increasingly dependent on the automobile in the early decades of the twentieth century and increasingly vulnerable to the transformations that dependence would bring.[69]

On Christmas Eve 1902, *The Scranton Times* included an article announcing "the biggest holiday trade in the history of Scranton."[70] Even in a year when Scrantonians, along with the rest of the region's populace, suffered through "America's most significant labor dispute," they apparently were able to purchase holiday gifts on an unprecedented scale. The article perhaps implies a resiliency of the people of northeastern Pennsylvania and the strength, at least temporarily, of the anthracite coal industry. The anthracite region, as a result of the labor peace established in the wake of the 1902 strike, would experience continued prosperity and the expansive growth of the coal industry until the end of World War I. The greatest year for anthracite was 1917–1918, when the industry produced about 100,000,000 tons of coal. But the prosperity, growth, and labor peace would not last long. Major strikes during the 1920s that interrupted the supply of coal, a lack of technological innovation by industry leaders, and increasing competition from oil and gas caused the demise of the anthracite industry.[71] In an insightful analysis of the region during the 1920s, Professor Sheldon Spear concludes: "A serious depression was destroying the prosperity of the anthracite region several years before the Great Depression struck the nation at large."[72] The days of "a big holiday trade" would soon disappear from the anthracite region for decades to come.

CHART 3
1890 POPULATION CHARACTERISTICS

	Total population	Total Foreign Born	Total Native Born Foreign Parents	Percent Foreign Born	Percent Foreign Born & Native Born Foreign Parents
Carbon	38,624	6,577	9,448	17%	24%
Lackawanna	142,088	46,367	54,760	33%	39%
Luzerne	201,203	64,078	66,017	32%	33%
Northumberland	74,698	9,526	10,967	13%	15%
Schuylkill	154,163	31,509	47,197	20%	31%
Total Population	610,776				
Total Foreign Born		158,055			
Total Native Born Foreign Parents			188,389		
Percent Foreign Born of Total Population					26%
Percent Foreign Born & Native Born Foreign Parents of Total Population					46%

CHART 4
1900 POPULATION CHARACTERISTICS

	Total population	Total Foreign Born	Total Native Born Foreign Parents	Percent Foreign Born	Percent Foreign Born & Native Born Foreign Parents
Carbon	44,510	7,275	11,202	16%	25%
Lackawanna	193,831	24,478	80,785	29%	42%
Luzerne	257,121	72,962	98,400	28%	38%
Northumberland	90,911	12,106	16,991	13%	17%
Schuylkill	172,927	32,668	53,370	19%	31%
Total Population	759,300				
Total Foreign Born		180,738			
Total Native Born Foreign Parents			260,748		
Percent Foreign Born of Total Population					24%
Percent Foreign Born & Native Born Foreign Parents of Total Population					58%

Notes

1. "New Year in Town,"*Wilkes-Barre Record*, Wednesday, 1 Jan 1902, 8; "The Weather," *Pottsville Daily Republican*, Wednesday, 1 Jan 1902, 1; "Terrible Floods Cause Havoc," *Wilkes-Barre Record*, Monday, 16 Dec 1901, 1; "Heavy Rains Cause Floods,"*Wilkes-Barre Record*, Tuesday, 31 Dec 1901, 1

2. "Exit 1901, Enter 1902," *Wilkes-Barre Record*, Wednesday, 1 Jan 1902, 8.

3. "A Happy New Year to All" *Pottsville Daily Republican*, Wednesday, 1 Jan 1902, 1.

4. "New Year in Town," *Wilkes-Barre Record*, Wednesday, 1 Jan 1902, 8; "A Happy New Year to All," *Pottsville Daily Republican*, Wednesday, 1 Jan 1902, 1.

5. Assemblies emerged as part of the custom of formally presenting young women to society, announcing them "ready-for-marriage." Historically, a young woman was introduced by her parents at a private party that marked the beginning of a year of dances, parties, teas, and various other events given in her honor. As time passed, group presentations of debutantes at elaborate balls became popular. A classic description of an Assembly Ball is found in Jane Austen's *Pride and Prejudice* published in 1813. For classic-film buffs, see *Pride and Prejudice* (1940) starring Laurence Olivier, Greer Garson, and Maureen O'Sullivan.

6. "The Close of the Social Year in Pottsville," *Pottsville Daily Republican*, Tuesday, 31 Dec 1901, 1.

7. For the best analysis of the character and changing status of a social and economic elite of Pottsville, see Edward J. Davies II, *The Anthracite Aristocracy: Leadership and Social Change in the Hard Coal Regions of Northeastern Pennsylvania, 1800–1930* (DeKalb, Ill: Northern Illinois University Press, 1985).

8. "The Assembly Ball," *Wilkes-Barre Record*, Wednesday, 1 Jan 1902, 3.

9. "The New Year," *Wilkes-Barre Record*, Wednesday, 1 Jan 1902, 6.

10. "A Happy New Year," *Pottsville Daily Republican*, Wednesday, 1 Jan 1902, 6.

11. Alfred D. Chandler, Jr., "Anthracite Coal and the Beginning of the Industrial Revolution in the United States," *Business History Review* 46 (1972): 179.

12. Edmund Morris, *Theodore Rex* (New York: Random House, 2001), 131.

13. Ibid.

14. Perry K. Blatz, "Titanic Struggles, 1873–1916" in Howard Harris, *Keystone of Democracy: A History of Pennsylvania Workers, ed. and assoc. ed. Perry K. Blatz* (Harrisburg: Commonwealth of Pennsylvania, Pennsylvania Historical and Museum, 1999), 86.

15. Donald L. Miller and Richard E. Sharpless, *The Kingdom of Coal: Work, Enterprise, and Ethnic Communities in the Mine Fields* (Philadelphia: University of Pennsylvania Press, 1985), 282.

16. For short, yet practical summaries of the Progressive Era, see George Brown Tindall and David E. Shi, *America: A Narrative History* (New York: W.W. Norton & Company, 1996), 1004–1022; and David M. Kennedy et al., *The Brief American Pageant: A History of the Republic* (New York: Houghton Mifflin Company, 2000), 426–438.

17. Richard Hofstadter, ed., *The Progressive Movement, 1900–1915* (Englewood Cliffs, N.J.: Prentice-Hall, 1963), 2–3.

18. Norman Davies, *Europe: A History* (New York: Oxford University Press, 1996), 763.

19. Jacques Barzun, *From Dawn to Decadence: 500 Years of Western Cultural Life, 1500 to the Present* (New York: Harper Collins Publishers, 2000), 683. See also *Paris Expo Pages: The Beautiful Time*, available at http://www.paris.org/Expos/BelleEpoque/be.html.

20. *Eras of Elegance: The Edwardian Era, 1901–1910*, available at http://www.erasofelegance.com/edwardian.html.

21. See Sordoni Art Gallery, *Vale of Wyoming: Nineteenth Century Images from Campbell's Ledge to Nanticoke* (Wilkes-Barre: Sordoni Art Gallery, Wilkes College,

1985); Irwin Richman, "Susquehanna's Painters," *Pennsylvania Heritage* XX Number 4 (1994): 7–17; Gilbert S. McClintock, *Valley Views of Northeastern Pennsylvania* (Princeton: Princeton University Press, 1948).

22. *Vale of Wyoming*, 27–30; "Susquehanna's Painters," 7–8; *Valley Views*, 28–29, 40.

23. Peter Roberts, *Anthracite Coal Communities* (New York: Arno Press and the New York Times, reprinted edition 1970), 6–10.

24. Hudson Coal Company, *The Story of Anthracite* (New York: The Hudson Coal Company, 1932), 12–13; Patrick W. O'Bannon et al., *Anthracite Coal in Pennsylvania: An Industry and a Region* (Harrisburg: Commonwealth of Pennsylvania, Bureau for Historic Preservation, Pennsylvania Historical and Museum Commission, 1997), 3.

25. John G. Clark et al., *Three Generations in Twentieth Century America: Family, Community, and Nation* (Homewood, Illinois: The Dorsey Press, 1977), 51–53; Richard Lingeman, *Small Town America: A Narrative History 1620–The Present* (Boston: Houghton Mifflin Company, 1980), 327; United States Census Bureau, "Table 1. Urban and Rural Population: 1900–1990," 6. Available at http://www.census.gov/population/censusdata/urpop0090.txt.

26. Burton W. Folsom Jr., *Urban Capitalists: Entrepreneurs and City Growth in Pennsylvania's Lackawanna and Lehigh Regions, 1800–1920* (Scranton: The University of Scranton Press, 2001), 113; *U.S. Census Bureau, 1900–1990, Population of the 100 Largest Cities and Other Urban Places in the United States: 1790 to 1990, Working Paper No. 27; 1996, "Estimates of the Population of Cities with Populations of 100,000 and Greater,"* available at http://www.census.gov/population/estimates/metro-city/SC100K96.txt.

27. Census data for 1890 and 1900 are from the *United States Historical Census Data Browser,* available at http://fisher.lib.virginia.edu/census.

28. *United States Historical Census Data Browser,* available at: http://fisher.lib.virginia.edu/census; Roberts, 19–21.

29. "An Atrocious Crime," *Wilkes-Barre Record,* Thursday, 27 Feb 1902, 3.

30. Robert A. Janosov, "Parochial Education History," HUD HOME Program: St. Gabriel's Convent & School Project, Hazleton, Luzerne County, Pennsylvania, BHP Reference Number: ER 97-0679-079-P (Harrisburg: Bureau for Historic Preservation, 2000), 5, 12; Thompson's *City Directory of Wilkes-Barre for 1902* (Wilkes-Barre: Journal of Commerce Publishing Company & Raeder Printing Company, 1902), 351–352; Rev. John P. Gallagher, *A Century of History: The Diocese of Scranton, 1868–1968* (Scranton: The Diocese of Scranton, 1968), 152–153.

31. "The Diamond City," *Board of Trade Journal* (Wilkes-Barre: Wilkes-Barre Board of Trade, April 1906), 4.

32. For a complete history of the street-railway system, see Thomas F. Flanagan, *Scranton Railway Company* (West Chester, PA: Ben Rohrbeck Publications, 1979).

33. For a complete analysis of Pottsville's decline as an urban leader in the anthracite region, see Davies, *The Anthracite Aristocracy,* 102–127.

34. "Greater Wilkes-Barre," *Board of Trade Journal* (Wilkes-Barre: January 1906), 4.

35. Thompson's *Wilkes-Barre City Directory for 1902,* 344–345; *United States Historical Census Data Browser,* available at http://fisher.lib.virginia.edu/census; Robert A. Janosov, *A Preliminary Survey of Wyoming Valley's Historic Anthracite Sites* (Wilkes-Barre: Historic Preservation Society of Luzerne County, n.d.), 12–13, 16.

36. *Report to the President on the Anthracite Coal Strike of May–October, 1902, by the Anthracite Coal Commission* (Washington, DC: Government Printing Office, 1903), 56; *Report of the Department of Mines of Pennsylvania, Part IB Anthracite, 1923–1924* (Harrisburg: Pennsylvania Department of Mines, 1927), 18.

37. Thompson's *Wilkes-Barre City Directory for 1902,* 354–357;

38. *The Scranton and Wilkes-Barre Society Blue Book* (New York: Dau Publishing Company, 1900), 51–76; Oscar Jewell Harvey and Ernest Gray Smith, *A History of Wilkes-Barre, Luzerne County, Pennsylvania* (Wilkes-Barre: Reader Press,

1909–1930), Vol. V, 213; *Walk Wilkes-Barre: A Self-Guided Tour of the Historic Center of Wilkes-Barre, Pennsylvania* (Wilkes-Barre: Wyoming Historical & Geological Society, 1999).

39. Robert A. Janosov, *Cold and Gold from the Poconos: A History of the Stegmaier Brewing Company, Wilkes-Barre, PA* (Nanticoke, PA: Tres Canis Publishing Company, 1997), 28.

40. Thompson's *Wilkes-Barre City Directory for 1902*, 354–357; *Wilkes-Barre Record Almanac for 1903* (Wilkes-Barre: The Wilkes-Barre Record, 1903), 33; Janosov, *Cold and Gold*, 25; "Consumption of Beer," *Wilkes-Barre Record*, 14 March 1902; "A Shock to Saloon Men," *Wilkes-Barre Record*, 25 Feb 25 1902.

41. *Wilkes-Barre Record Almanac for 1903* (Wilkes-Barre: The Wilkes-Barre Record, 1903), 26–27, 32–33; Thompson's *Wilkes-Barre City Directory for 1902* (Wilkes-Barre: Journal of Commerce Publishing Company & Raeder Printing Company, 1902), 344–345.

42. F. Charles Petrillo, *Harvey's Lake* (Wilkes-Barre: Wyoming Historical and Geological Society, 1991), 31.

43. C. Charles Ciesla, *History of Sans Souci Park, 1893–1973* (Hanover Township, PA: self-published, Third Edition, 2002), 18–19.

44. "In the Good Old Summertime," lyrics available at: http://my.execpc.com/~suden/goodold_summertime.html.

45. "Fought Fire with Fire," *Wilkes-Barre Record*, 25 April 1902.

46. Lawrence Squeri, *Better in the Poconos: The Story of Pennsylvania's Vacationland* (University Park, PA: The Pennsylvania State University Press, 2002), 62–77.

47. "A Day with the Circus," *Wilkes-Barre Record*, 20 May 1902.

48. *Wilkes-Barre Record Almanac for 1903* (Wilkes-Barre: The Wilkes-Barre Record, 1903), 78–79.

49. See William C. Kashatus, *Diamonds in the Coalfields: 21 Remarkable Baseball Players, Managers, and Umpires for Northeast Pennsylvania* (Jefferson, NC: McFarland & Company, Inc., 2002).

50. "New Building for Globe Store," *Wilkes-Barre Record*, 29 Jan 1902.

51. *Wilkes-Barre Record Almanac for 1903* (Wilkes-Barre: The Wilkes-Barre Record, 1903), 42–43, 86.

52. *Wilkes-Barre Record Almanac for 1903* (Wilkes-Barre: The Wilkes-Barre Record, 1903), 37–39.

53. Lackawanna Heritage Valley Steering Committee, *Plan for the Lackawanna Heritage Valley* (April 1991): 26; Folsom, *Urban Capitalists*, 24.

54. Daniel K. Perry, *A Fine Substantial Piece of Masonry: Scranton's Historic Furnaces* (Harrisburg: Commonwealth of Pennsylvania, Pennsylvania Historical and Museum Commission, 1994), 22–26.

55. Folsom, *Urban Capitalists*, 46–47.

56. University of Minnesota, Department of History, "Scranton Metropolitan Area, 1880–1940," available at: http://www.hist.umn.edu/~gardner/metro/md_Scranton.html. The communities included in the "urban fringe" group are: the boroughs of Blakely, Dickson City, Dunmore, Old Forge, Olyphant, Taylor, Throop, Winton and Old Forge Township; "outer fringe" communities include the city of Carbondale, the boroughs of Archbald, Jermyn, Mayfield, Moosic, Vandling, Forest City and the townships of Carbondale, Fell, Lackawanna, and South Abington.

57. Folsom, *Urban Capitalists*, 49–50, 91–92, 114–117; *United States Historical Census Data Browser*, available at: http://fisher.lib.virginia.edu/census; *The Scranton Times Annual for 1903* (Scranton: The Scranton Times Printery, 1903), 91.

58. *United States Historical Census Data Browser*, available at: http://fisher.lib.virginia.edu/census; *Williams' Scranton City Directory 1902* (Scranton: Williams Directory Company).

59. Lackawanna Heritage Valley Steering Committee, *Plan*, 29, 39.

60. Gallagher, A Century of History, 227–234.

61. The Scranton Times Annual for 1903, 45.

62. Flanagan, Scranton Railway Company, 7–8; The Scranton Times Annual for 1903, 90; Clay McShane, Down the Asphalt Path: The Automobile and the American City (New York: Columbia University Press, 1994), 115.

63. Williams' Scranton City Directory 1902, 16–31, 44–49, 53–55; Janosov, "Parochial Education History," 12–13.

64. Williams' Scranton City Directory 1902, 53–55; Rev. John Gallagher, A Century of History, 208–209, 277–278.

65. The Scranton Times Annual for 1903, 43–51; The Scranton Republican Almanac for 1903 (Scranton: J.A. Scranton and Son, 1903), 5–27.

66. The Scranton Times Annual for 1903, 43–51; William C. Kashatus, 78.

67. The Scranton Times Annual for 1903, 43–51; The Scranton Republican Almanac for 1903, 5–27.

68. Public Roads Administration, Highway Statistics: Summary to 1945 (Washington, DC: U.S. Government Printing Office, 1947), 18–27, 73; Thomas J. Schlereth, Victorian America Transformations in Everyday Life, 1876–1915 (New York: Harper Collins, 1991), 25; City of Scranton, 1926 Annual Report of the Public Works Department (Scranton: City of Scranton, 1926).

69. For a complete consideration of the automobile and transformation of American society, see McShane, Down the Asphalt Path.

70. The Scranton Times Annual for 1903, 51.

71. O'Bannon et al., Anthracite Coal in Pennsylvania, 81–83.

72. Sheldon Spear, "High Noon Or Twilight?", Proceedings of the Fourth Annual Conference on the History of Northeastern Pennsylvania: The Last 100 Years (Nanticoke, PA: Luzerne County Community College, 1992), 89.

The "Faces" of John Mitchell: News Coverage of the Great Anthracite Strike of 1902 in the Regional and National Press

Joseph P. McKerns

It had "legs." It had "heart." And, it could leave you with "chills." To journalists of the time, it was everything a great news story should be. The Great Anthracite Strike of 1902, with its drama, conflict and hardship, played out before the eyes of the American reading public in daily newspapers across the United States from May through October 1902. Considered a benchmark in labor history today, the strike was the biggest and longest-running news story of the year. In fact, the strike's "legs" carried the story from early 1901, when issues left unresolved by the Strike of 1900 brought labor and capitalism to the brink of confrontation, to early 1903 and the conclusion of the Anthracite Strike Commission hearings. The strike was front page news, not only in the local press and newspapers in the big cities nearby, such as Philadelphia and New York, but in major daily newspapers as far away as the *Chicago Tribune*, the *Atlanta Constitution*, and the *San Francisco Chronicle*. Newspapers nationwide carried reports nearly daily throughout the period of the strike, sometimes running two, three, or more stories in a single edition. Granted, some of these stories were supplied by the Associated Press news service, but the many of the stories were tagged "Special to the ….", indicating that the paper had its own reporter on the scene.

Besides having all the elements of a great news story, it also had a cast of players worthy of a drama: the poor and downtrodden (the miners), the evil dukes and barons (the coal operators), the handsome young prince (John Mitchell), and the noble and wise king (Theodore Roosevelt). And, hovering above it all, J. Pierpont Morgan, like Zeus looking down from Olympus, waiting to see if he should intercede and on whose behalf. Robert Wiebe was right, it was a morality play.[1]

While the strike was clearly a benchmark in the history of labor in the United States, it also may be considered a benchmark in the history of American journalism, and not only for the obvious reason that it was one of the first times much of the nation's daily press sympathized with the strikers in a labor-management dispute, but for several less obvious, but perhaps more important reasons. Fully two decades before the term "public relations" was first used,[2] and a half-century before the term "news management" was coined,[3] the great coal strike showed that something very much like these practices were at play.

THE REAL OBJECT OF THE OPERATORS IS TO CRUSH IT.

From the *Ohio State Journal* (Columbus).

Following the 1902 strike, editorial cartoons from across the country were compiled into one volume. The hammer wielded by the "operators" above reads "No Concessions, No Arbitration, No Interference."

Courtesy of the Ohio State University Department of History

The consensus among historians of the strike was that the press played a major role in shaping public opinion about the strike, which in turn influenced the way the strike was resolved.[4] In fact, that the press had an impact is assumed. There is little, if any, real analysis of why and how the press had an impact. Yes, the studies cite representative newspaper editorials from around the nation, but that approach misses an important point, i.e., the "devil is in the details." The thesis of this paper is that the impact of the press lay more in how it told the story of the strike in the news columns, than what it said the story meant in its editorials. The "how" of the news involved more than facts, it included the way the facts were framed, the way the stories were structured, and the words chosen to describe what the reporter saw. If news is a window on the world, then the way the window is made matters. This paper examines a sampling of news stories gleaned from the newspapers of the coal region and the nation. It is a report of a first foray into this subject and is admittedly preliminary, exploratory, and somewhat speculative. The news stories were read and analyzed for the way they presented the facts, and not for the facts themselves.

The Press in 1902

The daily newspaper in America was near the peak of its evolution in 1902. It was the main source of news for the nation's people, i.e., at least 26 percent of the nation's population subscribed to a newspaper. Many readers regularly purchased more than one daily, depending on the news. The newspapers reached every stratum of society, poor and rich, working class and aristocrat, rural and urban, small town and big city, as well as the highly educated and those who were barely literate or who needed to have the news read to them. There were approximately 2,000 daily newspapers in the United States, 1,000 foreign-language newspapers, and more than 12,000 weekly newspapers. There were newspapers for African Americans, for every ethnic group, and every religious denomination, and even some not affiliated with any religion at all.[5]

The practice of journalism was in a state of transition in 1902. While not yet a self-conscious "profession" that espoused the ideal of "objectivity" in reporting the news, it was a practice on its way to becoming a profession. Editors wanted facts because facts made up news stories, and news stories sold papers. Competition between papers was intense. Most cities of any size had at least two competing daily newspapers. Many had three, four or more. The nation's biggest cities, such as New York and Chicago, had a dozen dailies. In such a close climate, beating your competition with the latest news could mean the difference between the paper's life and death in the marketplace.[6] Circulation and advertising were the blood and the veins of the newspaper business. Big news stories, not editorials, brought readers to the paper. The simple fact was that newspaper design in the early 1900s was intended to spur circulation by attracting readers to the "news" first, which also exposed readers to the advertisements on the news pages, and editorial comment second.[7] The larger the type size and the higher up the page a story appeared conveyed the importance, drama and excitement of the news. The editorial pages were often just a mass of gray type with few headlines that caught the eye. A reader had to look for the editorials; the news stories jumped out at them. And when the news stories had a human face, as they did during the strike of 1902, that was a bonus. Putting a "face" on the facts helped the reader identify with the story. In the strike of 1902, that face belonged to John Mitchell.

John Mitchell and the Press

John Mitchell seemed to be at the center of many of the strike stories. Either he had a remarkably natural and intuitive sense of the importance of "presence" in the public eye, or he keenly understood what to say, and how to act in order to get the press to tell his story the way he wanted it told. For Mitchell, like Roosevelt, who was the most media-savvy president up to that time, it was probably a mixture of both. Unfortunately the coal operators, in particular George F. Baer, were lacking in both. Not only did the operators display a gross lack of tact in their arrogant comments to the press, it wasn't the best of times to be a plutocrat in America. A national wave of reform journalism burst onto the public stage in the early 1900s, with its target very often being industrialists and their unfair business practices. This wave of journalism would later be labeled "muckraking," a term coined in 1906 by none other than Theodore Roosevelt. It was a bad time to be a "robber baron."[8]

It seems that all the principal players in the strike realized that the press would be an important factor in the strike's outcome. Public figures, most notably President Roosevelt himself, understood that control of information aided in achieving policy goals.[9] Since the newspapers were the best and most efficient means of reaching a mass public, or any part of it, the more control exerted over the information newspapers printed, the better. A newspaper could oppose a public figure in its editorial columns, but still have to publish positive information about the person in its news columns. Additionally, changes in the way reporters gathered news in the quarter-century preceding the strike made managing the news easier for public figures. Reporters came to rely more on getting information from authoritative sources than on first-hand observation. Also, the practice of quoting sources verbatim, and of publishing interviews with sources became widespread. Both of these practices enhanced public figures' control of information. It may be safe to speculate at this point that Mitchell, like Roosevelt, seemed to have a fine appreciation for the way news was made and how to use that to his advantage.[10]

Modern-day public relations professionals speak about reaching *"publics"* with their messages, implying that their target is seldom a singular one, but instead is a multiplicity of varied targets, each one requiring a separate, tailor-made message. John Mitchell demonstrated, at least in the news stories about the strike examined here, that he understood his publics to be multiple, i.e. 1) mine workers in general and the rank and file of the UMWA in particular; 2) the general American public; 3) government, especially national government and public officials; 4) the coal operators; and 5) the Wall Street financiers who were the power behind the coal industry. Mitchell seemed to fashion his message to reach the appropriate public at the appropriate time. Even his often-mentioned conservatism, his habit of dressing in the manner of a priest, even the fact that he was, like most Roman Catholic priests of the time, clean-shaven could be seen as part of a communication strategy intended to highlight the message that he was different than what the public might expect a labor leader to be like. He aimed to place himself in a favorable light when contrasted with the reactionary, arrogant stance of the coal operators, who looked and sounded like aristocrats. If Mitchell was the "face" the press chose to put on the strike, then the face that Mitchell showed depended on who his target public was.

The "Faces" of John Mitchell

What follows is an analysis of selected news stories from local, regional, and national newspapers published during three important phases of the strike, i.e., 1) the beginning of the strike; 2) the dates surrounding the Shenandoah riots, roughly mid-point in the strike; and 3) the end of the strike.

The Strike Is On!

Months before the UMW strike began, John Mitchell seemed to be using the press to disseminate messages to various "publics." During the Shamokin convention in March 1902, Mitchell sent a message of caution and careful consideration:

> President Mitchell said he addressed the convention and advised caution and prudence in arriving at a decision as to further action. He reviewed efforts made by officers of the union to maintain peace and harmony in the coal regions by adoption of humane measures and the best methods of adjusting wage differences.[11]

This statement may have been aimed at the general public, fearful that the miners would seize upon the slightest pretext to go out on strike. It also conveys that all the miners wanted were "humane measures." Furthermore, Mitchell's statement pointed a finger of blame in the direction of the operators: Note that it is the "employees" to whom the operators refuse to respond, not John Mitchell.

UNCLE SAM: "I wonder how much longer that fellow can stand it!"—From the *Journal* (Detroit).

Mitchell's success in securing public support is evident in the cartoons on these pages, where the mine operators are portrayed unsympathetically.

All images courtesy of the Ohio State University Department of History

A BURNING QUESTION.—From the *Plain Dealer* (Cleveland).

FOLLOWING A HIGH EXAMPLE.
" The Coal Trust has just had its photograph taken in the graceful attitude of jumping a high fence on horseback."— From the *Journal* (New York).

He also spoke of the failure of the operators to respond to the employees' overtures.[12]

Three days later, Mitchell continued as the voice of calm and reason after the convention was told that the operators had sent a communication indicating they would not bargain with the miners:

> ... the delegates, after the contents of the operators' letters were made known, were emphatic in declaring for recognition at any cost, but conservative counsel by Mitchell calmed the storm and changed the sentiment...[13]

In the same news story, someone, probably Mitchell since he is the only union official quoted in the story, uses a technique commonly employed by news sources today who want a message to go out, but don't want to be pinned down by it, i.e., the anonymous source:

> No strike will be ordered by the present convention and no time limit will, it is asserted on the highest authority, be placed on either of the prospective committees to conclude negotiations.[14]

The phrase "on the highest authority" is usually reserved for use with an anonymous source who is a head of state, or highest official of an organization or business.

At the Hazleton convention of the UMWA in mid-May, Mitchell's statement that he would leave the question of whether or not to strike up to the miners themselves was greeted with editorial approval by the local press:

RESTS WITH THE RANK AND FILE OF THE MINERS.

> National President Mitchell, the district presidents and the executive boards of the United Mine Workers came to a wise conclusion when they decided at Scranton last week to submit the question of a strike or no strike to a direct vote of the miners.[15]

On the eve of the strike vote, Mitchell gave an interview to the *Boston Evening Transcript* in which he said "he would advise the miners what course to pursue when the proper time comes." Furthermore, during the interview with the *Transcript*, Mitchell said that even though "all negotiations with the mine-owners are off," he may try to delay any action "in the hope that something may come from the other side."[16]

When the convention voted for a strike three days later, the *Pottsville Miners' Journal* front-page news story noted that Mitchell remained the advocate of peace, even though he would carry out the will of the rank and file:

> With Mitchell on the peace side, the only thing that invoked a strike was the definite instructions given to so many delegates.[17]

The story also related that "it was learned ... several counter proposals to a general strike were made." This information comes in the second sentence of a paragraph containing a statement by Mitchell in which he refused to discuss what the convention had considered prior to the strike vote. Contemporary journalists refer to this type of anonymous information as "background," meaning that it can be used but not attributed to any source whatsoever. This statement seemed aimed at assuring the general public that calmer voices may yet prevail.

Four days after the strike vote, Mitchell made another statement to the press apparently aimed at the general public. Many newspapers gave it a treatment similar to that of the *Atlanta Constitution*:

COAL OPERATORS
HIS ONLY FOES

Mitchell Says His Quarrel
Is with Them Alone

Doesn't Want Anybody to Suffer
Except the Operators[18]

The story quoted Mitchell verbatim:

> ... I will say that we do not desire to make any city a victim or have any person suffer because of our quarrel with the coal companies.[19]

Nevertheless, Mitchell said in an interview with the *Pottsville Miners' Journal* that he believed the nation's bituminous miners would be justified in breaking agreements with soft-coal operators if it meant aiding the union's cause, thus raising the specter of a massive strike that could paralyze the nation. This statement covers several publics: It tells the miners that he's willing to do whatever is necessary to win the strike; it also warns those who might interpret his "man of peace" stance as a weakness that neither the strike, nor John Mitchell, are to be taken lightly.[20]

Riot and Bloodshed in Shenandoah

The lowest point of the strike for John Mitchell must have come on the afternoon of July 30 when miners in Shenandoah attacked two men they believed were "scabs." The miners' rage turned into bloodshed that left a shop owner beaten to death on the streets. Newspaper estimates of the number of miners involved ranged from 800 to 5,000. If there was one thing Mitchell would not have wanted to happen, it was the loss of life, especially that of any person not involved in the strike in any way. The regional and national press played the "riot and bloodshed" angle very large:

A FATAL RIOT

–Hazleton Daily Standard [21]

SCORES ARE SHOT
IN MINE BATTLE

–Chicago Tribune [22]

NATIONAL GUARD AT SHENANDOAH
WILD MOB CREATES REIGN OF TERROR AT THAT PLACE

–Harrisburg Telegraph [23]

BLOOD SPOUTING IN COAL REGIONS
AND TROOPS HURRY TO THE SCENE

–Atlanta Constitution [24]

ARMED TROOPS ON GUARD
IN SHENANDOAH STREETS

–New York Evening Journal [25]

EXTENSIVE RIOTING AT
SHENANDOAH LAST NIGHT,
TROOPS HAVE ARRIVED

–Wilkes-Barre Times [26]

The national guard troops ordered into Shenandoah had a quieting effect, but Mitchell was also quick to respond to the crisis. Mitchell assured the American public that his efforts to maintain peace "will be redoubled."[27] Furthermore, he was emphatic in stressing that he had warned the miners that any person who violated the law "was the worst enemy the strikers could have,"[28] thereby bidding to enlist the miners themselves in maintaining order. Also, Mitchell let it be known that he had replied to an open letter from the Citizens' Alliance of Wilkes-Barre which asked him to "issue a proclamation" to the miners "warning them to keep on the side of law and order" by asserting that he "had always been a staunch defender of law and order and that his followers know it."[29]

Following his reassurances that he and the union would maintain the peace, Mitchell rallied the rank and file while serving notice to the coal operators that he was prepared to stay the course despite the setback at Shenandoah:

BATTLE TO LAST DITCH,
URGES JOHN MITCHELL

Strike Leader Declares
Miners Will Win if They
Are Firm [30]

The story reported his appearance before 7,000 miners in Scranton two days after the Shenandoah riot, amidst rumors in the local and national press that the strikers were distressed by the violence and tiring of the strike. The *Atlanta Constitution* reported that the miners "went fairly wild over Mitchell."[31] The paper described the scene of his speech while quoting Mitchell at length:

> "It has been said by some men who are not your friends that the miners of Scranton are getting tired of the strike and are about to return to work. I come to find out if this is so. I want to know if you are going to work, dishonoring your organization and dishonoring yourselves."
>
> Cries of "Never! Never!" "No, No," "Don't you believe it," and the like.
>
> "If the strike is lost, may God Almighty help the men, women and children who depend for their subsistence on the mining of anthracite coal. If the strike is lost, you will pay the cost of the strike.
>
> "I want to say that the anthracite miners went on strike themselves. It will never end until you vote it ended."[32]

Mitchell also let the miners and the coal operators know that he was still confident of success:

MITCHELL IS VERY SANGUINE

Says He Is Confident His Men Will
Win[33]

The Strike Is Declared Over

In the strike's final phase, Mitchell's primary target seemed to be a public of one—President Theodore Roosevelt. By winning over the popular president, Mitchell also may have been trying to reach out to a broader public—the respectable American middle class. He did this by showing the president and the public the "face" of a "gentleman businessman." Mitchell presented himself as everything the coal operators, with their wealth, education, and social standing, should have been but weren't. In the face of the coal operators' stubbornness, and open disrespect for the president, Mitchell was most respectful, open to negotiation, willing to compromise, and a gentleman in maintaining his composure when insulted by the operators. The newspapers painted a vivid picture for their readers, e.g.:

COAL BARONS LAUGH TO SCORN
PRESIDENT OF THE UNITED STATES

MINERS TRUST CASE
TO THE PRESIDENT[34]

The accompanying story printed the full text of the UMWA's statement that Mitchell and the union's representatives made to Roosevelt:

THE TWO MEN AT THE LEVER, OR HOW WE GOT COAL
—*Philadelphia North American*

While the operators (above, trying to close the gate of the coal hopper) continued to resist pressure to let the miners go back to work, Mitchell worked closely
with President Roosevelt to end the strike, earning praise from the public and
enhancing his reputation as a responsible leader of the working man..

Courtesy of the Ohio State University Department of History.

Conscious of the responsibility resting upon us, conscious of our duty to society, conscious of our obligations to the one hundred and fifty thousand miners we have the honor to represent, we have, after most careful consideration, and with the hope of relieving the situation and avoiding the sufferings and hardships which would probably follow in the wake of a coal famine, decided to propose a resumption of coal mining upon the lines hereinafter suggested.[35]

The statement conveys social responsibility, reasonableness, sensitivity, patriotism, and deference to the president. In a single stoke, Mitchell conveys a clear message to several publics. That it was effective may be implied from the response of ministers of mainstream Protestant churches in Chicago:

VOICE OF PULPIT
IN MINERS' CAUSE

Chicago Ministers Align Themselves
on the Side of the Strikers

SCORE THE COAL BARONS

President Roosevelt Course Is Praised
and John Mitchell Is Commended [36]

Conclusion

The preceding examples of newspaper coverage of the strike of 1902 seem to indicate that John Mitchell had a keen understanding of the workings of the press and how to use this knowledge to project an image or "face" that addressed the several publics affected by the strike. To the mine workers, he appeared strong, resolute, and firm, while remaining their advocate and representative, not their dictator. To the American public, he showed himself to be unlike what might be expected of a union official, i.e., he was responsible, sensitive to the public's concerns, and willing to find a solution that would serve the good of all, not just the union. To President Roosevelt he was the "gentleman businessman", a man of authority who accorded respect due those in higher authority. And to the coal operators, he was fearless, determined, and everything they should have been but weren't.

Notes

1. Robert H. Wiebe, "The Anthracite Strike of 1902: A Record of Confusion," *Mississippi Valley Historical Review* 48:2 (Sept. 1961), 229.

2. Jean Folkerts and Dwight L. Teeter, Jr., *Voices of a Nation: A History of Mass Media in the United States*, 3rd ed. (Boston: Allyn and Bacon, 1998), 271.

3. Ibid., 484.

4. For example, this is the conclusion arrived at by Wiebe, "The Anthracite Strike of 1902," 241, and Robert J. Cornell, *The Anthracite Coal Strike of 1902* (Washington, D.C.: Catholic University of America Press, 1957), 143–172.

5. Folkerts and Teeter, *Voices of a Nation*, 251–252.

6. Ibid., 243–246.

7. Ibid., 253–271. Editorial pages then, as now, were "ad-less."

8. Ibid., 306–310.

9. A discussion of Roosevelt's press relations is found throughout Edmund Morris, *Theodore Rex* (New York: Random House, 2001).

10. This comment is based solely on a reading of the news stories on the strike. A thorough search of the Mitchell Papers at the Catholic University of America in Washington, D.C., and other appropriate records of the United Mine Workers of America is necessary to confirm or qualify it.

11. *Scranton Republican*, 21 March 1902, 1.

12. Ibid.

13. *Scranton Republican*, 24 March 1902, 1.

14. Ibid.

15. *Hazleton Plain Speaker*, 12 May 1902, 2.

16. *Boston Evening Transcript*, 15 May 1902, 2.

17. *Pottsville Miners' Journal*, 16 May 1902, 1.

18. *Atlanta Constitution*, 20 May 1902, 3.

19. Ibid.

20. *Pottsville Miners' Journal*, 20 May 1902, 1.

21. 31 July 1902, 1.

22. 31 July 1902, 1.

23. 31 July 1902, 1.

24. 31 July 1902, 1.

25. 31 July 1902, 1.

26. 31 July 1902, 1.

27. *Scranton Republican*, 1 August 1902, 1.

28. Ibid.

29. *Boston Evening Transcript*, 1 August 1902, 2.

30. *Atlanta Constitution*, 2 August 1902, 1.

31. Ibid.

32. Ibid.

33. *Atlanta Constitution*, 4 August 1902, 1.

34. *Atlanta Constitution*, 4 October 1902, 1.

35. Ibid.

36. *Chicago Tribune*, 6 October 1902, 2.

The Role of Intimidation and Violence in
The Great Anthracite Strike of 1902

Lance E. Metz

The Great Anthracite Strike of 1902 has long been perceived to be a relatively nonviolent labor dispute. The discouragement of violence by the leadership of the United Mine Workers of America was a conscious policy by its president, John Mitchell, to win both public sympathy for the miners' cause and support from business leaders, political bosses, the general public, and influential organizations such as the National Civic Foundation.[1] Mitchell was a conservative leader, and he was more willing to negotiate with opponents than to confront them. However, did the reality of the 1902 anthracite strike match the widespread belief that it was a largely nonviolent affair? I believe that both the use of violence and the threat of intimidation by strikers was an essential part of the miners' eventual victory. Although few of the incidents that will be cited resulted in a large loss of life or property, it was their cumulative effect that prevented the operators from effectively reopening their mines using substitute labor. To gain the data needed to support my conclusion, I have examined strike coverage by a major regional paper, *The Allentown Morning Call*. Despite the fact that this source had an anti-labor bias, as did most newspapers of the time, I contend that it does represent an accurate picture of a strike, the success of which depended on intimidation and violence to insure that the collieries stayed shut. Success would deprive urban markets of the anthracite that was needed for both industrial and domestic use, thus generating a public demand to settle the strike.

The Allentown Morning Call employed a number of special correspondents to cover the 1902 strike and for its entire duration the events of this labor stoppage occupied the paper's daily front page from May thru October. On May 13, *The Call* wrote of the newly found solidarity of the anthracite miners:

> No better illustration of the numerical strength which the United Mine Workers organization has developed in the last two years could be shown than the practical unanimity with which the order of the executive board was obeyed.
>
> In the summer of 1900 the miners, laborers and breaker boys of the Lackawanna and Wyoming fields laid down their tools promptly and effectively, but the workers in the Lehigh and Schuylkill districts obeyed the strike order reluctantly in many sections and not at all in others. Probably 30,000 employees obeyed the summons of two years ago. Today fully twice that number paid no attention to the shrill blasts of the colliery whistles.[2]

Breaker boys at the Ewen Colliery of the Pennsylvania Coal Company, 1913.
Courtesy of F. Charles Petrillo.

Clearly the maintenance of the strikers' solidarity was, by the mine laborers, to be the key to victory. Without experienced workers the collieries
could not be operated or maintained. The use of implied threats and physical force to achieve this goal soon became an established feature of the 1902
strike. The operators realized this fact and attempted to counter it by con-
verting collieries into armed camps, by attempting to entice workers back to
work, and by hiring non-union workers from outside the anthracite region.[3]

The strikers' reaction to the hiring of non-union workers was both swift
and emphatic as was reported in the following *Morning Call* excerpt from
May 28:

> Several small disturbances occurred this morning at the mines where the
> non-union men are employed and where clerks and bosses are taking the
> place of firemen and pumpmen. None of them was at all serious.
>
> At the Woodward colliery of the Delaware Lackawanna and West-
> ern, a crowd of women and boys hooted the non-union men. At the Jer-
> sey colliery of the same company, where seventy men are fighting a fire,
> they had to run the gauntlet of an angry crowd, but no violence was at-
> tempted.
>
> In the Hazleton region, where non-union workers have been obtained
> at the Cranberry colliery and at other works where they are non-union
> employes, the men were hooted by crowds which followed them to the
> gates of the mines. This has already made many non-union men give up
> the work in fear of assault, while others are insisting that the companies
> house them at the mines and guard them with coal and iron police.[4]

By the end of May 1902, the stakes in the conflict had been considerably raised when the UMWA called out the fireman and engineers, who operated the pumps that kept the mines from flooding. The operators recognized that this action represented the most serious threat to their property, as one official of the Hillside Iron and Coal Company remarked to a *Morning Call* reporter, "The breakers could be rebuilt in six or eight months, but if the mine workers insist upon flooding these mines, it will take twice that long to get them in shape again."[5]

The tension in the anthracite coal regions was greatly exacerbated by the exodus of the pumpmen from the mines, and within a week violence occurred. The operators had greatly increased the ranks of the coal and iron policemen guarding their mines. Many of these men were unemployed urban toughs of Philadelphia and New York, whose relative lack of discipline made a volatile situation much worse, as related from the following confrontation that occurred near Pittston:

> The most serious disturbance of the present anthracite coal strike near occurred here at 11 o'clock this morning when miners attacked and badly beat John Williams, superintendent of the Erie colliery. Williams was injured and was carried inside the colliery. He was without medical attendance, for some time, as no physician would go to the place.
>
> The trouble grew out of the action of several coal and iron policemen who attacked a ten-year-old boy because he had ridiculed them. The lad was badly hurt and the strikers then gathered about colliery and attacked the policemen. It was in the scrimmage that followed that Williams was hurt. What the extent of his injuries were can not be learned as the colliery is guarded by deputies and no one is allowed to enter.[6]

Further violence was reported by the *Morning Call* at both Wilkes-Barre and the patch town of Mather's Mill:

> Rifle shots, the first heard since the strike of the 107,000 anthracite miners began this spring, came from the Empire colliery, of the Lehigh and Wilkes-Barre Coal Company, early this morning, when the coal and iron policemen on guard drove back a mob of men and boys who had threatened to burn the place.
>
> The shots were fired over the heads of the attacking party and did no damage. They served, however, to disperse the throng for the time being.
>
> The occurrence was reported to the police here by John Thomas, city scavenger. Mayor Price says he will have the affair investigated.
>
> For nearly thirty-six hours there has been a crowd around the Empire mine owing to the rumor that some of the imported colored laborers had been taken there.
>
> There was also a spectacular demonstration made this morning at Miner's Mill. Yesterday morning and last night there were slight disturbances in that town, but by far the most threatening move was made to-day, when the strikers met on a vacant lot at 5 o'clock.

They had spotted several men living near by who had remained at work either as engineers or pumpmen in the Dorrance and Pine Ridge collieries.

Most of these men slept behind the barracks in the mines, but two of them had ventured home last night and as they started for work they were promptly stopped by the crowd. They were allowed to go upon their promise not to attempt to return to work again.

Then the strikers prepared a stuffed figure, placarded with a threat against the men who were at work. This they carried at the head of their line and began a march to all the houses of non-union men. Stopping in front of these the strikers' fife and drum corps rattled off a dead march. Many of the strikers are Welshmen and in their native tongue they sang a dirge.

Cowering behind closed shutters the women in the families of the men at work watched the mob and trembled at the thought of what might come next. Before leaving each house the crowd yelled threats of all kinds and left written notices for the non-union men and their families to leave town. Also one at the house of William Martin, son of the sheriff, who was in charge of the deputies at the time of the Lattimer shooting.[7]

The following somewhat humorous episode illustrates the role that family loyalties played in the strike:

SCHOLARS ON STRIKE.

The crowd made the most hostile demonstration at the house of a man named Hoskins. The strikers met with a surprise, however. There was no one in the house but Hoskin's daughter, who is employed as a school teacher. She stepped boldly to the front door and said:

"I'm tired of having you men come around here and yell at me. This is the third time, and I wish you would stop it. You can't make my father stop work that way. He has a right to be at work. He does not belong to you, and I'm glad he is at work. Now go away and don't act like cowards."

The men in the crowd cheered her, but the boys did not like their teacher's spunk and promptly organized a strike. So, when she went to her school house later she found all her pupils in a lot playing ball, and they absolutely refused to enter the schoolroom.[8]

Another incident involving both striking mine workers and members of their families in attempts to keep the collieries closed is illustrated by the following incident at Plymouth:

A fight between strikers and non-union men occurred near the Delaware Lackawanna and Western depot here to-day. A score of non-union men were about to board a train that was to take them to a company mine to work. Several hundred men, women and children gathered about the depot and tried to keep the non-union men from the train. Children threw stones at them, and a desperate fight followed, the women participating. Coal and iron police rushed to the rescue of the non-unionists, and were roughly handled by the men. Several men were injured and two rioters were arrested.[9]

As the strike continued through the early summer, the collieries of the Coxe Brothers Company in southern Luzerne County became a focal point of violence, a distinction that they would maintain throughout the strike:

> Before dawn this morning about two hundred men from Merwinburg marched into Oneida, where Coxe Brothers and Company have a big colliery. There was some promiscuous shooting and considerable yelling, but no one was injured. A car carrying special policemen was sent from Drifton to the scene of the disturbance, but when the police got there the crowd had dispersed.[10]

From my study of these incidents, I have come to the conclusion that these incidents were either spontaneous or led by informal leaders while the elected officials of the UMWA made every attempt to prevent further outbreaks of violence and defuse those that developed. A case in point is the following incident from Drifton:

> The five special policemen, who were kidnapped by strikers at the railroad station upon their arrival from Philadelphia last night, returned home this morning in charge of J.P. Gallagher, district secretary of the United Mine Workers, who furnished the transportation.[11]

A coal and iron policeman, hired by coal operators to guard their property. Courtesy of the Schuylkill County Historical Society.

By June of 1902 the recruitment of coal and iron police was reaching large numbers as the operators attempted to both protect their property and overawe the strikers:

> Two carloads more of men from Philadelphia arrived here [Wilkes-Barre] to-day and were assigned to various mines. It would appear that there are at least 5,000 of these men in the region, and as not more than half of them are duly authorized to act as coal and iron police, the strikers are wondering what the other men are doing.[12]

Throughout June of 1902 a series of newspaper accounts showed that the strikers' tactics of intimidation and violence were continuing to have an effect:

> In the Jersey Mine, where a fire is raging, every man quit work this morning, leaving the property to burn. Till to-day the D. L. and W. Company had been enabled to keep about seventy men at work fighting the flames. These men lived at Plymouth, mostly at the lower end of the town. The lives of members and their families have been made so miserable of late that they decided to stop work this morning. The house of one of those men, John Musol, was mysteriously burned Sunday night. Wives of other workmen complained to their husbands that they heard threats against their houses.
>
> Three other collieries are known to be in distress. These are the Avondale, of the D. L. and W. Company, which is being rapidly flooded and threatens to cave in; No. 11, of the Lehigh and Wilkes-Barre Company, where the pumps have been broken by unskilled workmen, and where offers of five dollars a day have been vainly made for men, and No. 5, of the Susquehanna Coal Company, at Nanticoke, where shafts are flooding and gas accumulating at such a rate that warning notices have been posted.[13]

Weather was perceived by the strikers as a major factor in determining the outcome of this labor dispute. With the general inability of the operators to man the drainage pumps, mines could be flooded by rainstorms and numerous cave-ins could also occur as the *Morning Call*'s reporter wrote from Pottsville:

> All the working people in the mining region are praying for rain. This, they consider, would be the greatest help they could get toward winning their battle. The mines have little water in them but if there is a heavy rainfall, promptly followed by very warm weather the striking workingmen assert this will knock out the green hands who are working in the fire rooms and about the engines. They say that the rush of water will give the pumps more than the non-union engineers can handle and that with very warm weather the inexperienced fireman will suffer so much from the heat that they will be unable to stick at their work.[14]

As the strike wore on the use of hanging effigies became a powerful symbol of the strikers' solidarity and a potent warning to non-union workers to stay out of their mines:

Notwithstanding the union's order against the hanging of effigies, this diversion caused serious disturbances at Duryea and Pittston this morning. The hanging of these figures last night caused trouble with the telephone service and repair gangs were sent out this morning.

A crowd of Italians at Duryea attacked the repair gang and forced the telephone men to rehang the effigies on poles after removing them from the wires. At Parsonage street, Pittston, a similar scene occurred.[15]

The Pennsylvania Coal Company's N. 14 Colliery in Pittston Township. Courtesy of Robert P. Wolensky

As violence and threats continued to be evident in the anthracite coal regions during June 1902, the operators resorted to innovative means to identify the individuals who attempted to attack their collieries under the cover of darkness.

Huge photographic cameras and heavy loads of flashlight powders are to be installed as a part of the defenses of Fort Susquehanna at Nanticoke.

Colliery No. 5, at Nanticoke, or Fort Susquehanna, as it is called, has been fortified and garrisoned by the operators in a manner truly military and is in the charge of a young lieutenant, who served in the Cuban campaign, and who is a graduate of Yale. He has provided for the protection of the colliery in a manner to excite the admiration of military authorities and now to the barbed wire entanglements, moats and stockades with eighty armed men and a thousand feet of heavy fire hose, he has added a battery of cameras.

It is the intention of Lieutenant Jones to have several professional photographers in readiness at the colliery to take a number of photographs of any crowd that attempts to make an attack of any sort on the coal fort.[16]

In the cities of the anthracite coal regions the strikers received much-needed support from other labor organizations and working men. This solidarity helped to create in the public mind a perception of an impending coal crisis:

> Whatever may be the condition of the coal market in places outside of this region, a crisis is at hand in Wilkes-Barre, Scranton, Hazleton and other cities. The teamsters positively refuse to carry a pound of coal for any purpose.
>
> Many business men laid in large stocks of coal and left it lying in yards near their buildings. Now they find that it might as well be at the North Pole. As an instance, the leading hotel here has one hundred tons stored in a lot owned by the proprietor. He can not get a pound of this without starting a riot and a boycott. So the hotel is unable to secure power to run its electric lighting plant and elevators.
>
> Scores of business houses are in similar plight, and from interviews with many of these men it is learned that next week will witness a wholesale stoppage of factories throughout northeastern Pennsylvania.
>
> Men try to keep silent under their misfortune for fear of a boycott.[17]

The costs of attempting to maintain and protect the collieries began to take an increasingly heavy financial toll on the operators. This growing burden is clearly evident in the following segment of a *Morning Call* article filed from Wilkes-Barre:

> Attempts were made to secure something like exact information from several mine superintendents to-day regarding the extent of the operators' losses since the strike began. All of the men questioned took the position that the public is incurring a huge bill that must be paid out of next winter's coal money. The superintendents say the losses to the operators come from three sources; first, the wages paid to unproductive labor; second, the damage going done to the mines by flooding; third, the loss of trade to bituminous dealers, and the loss upon 250,000 idle coal cars.
>
> In the line of unproductive labor the operators are now supporting four thousand firemen, pumpmen and engineers at unusually high rates of wages. They are paying five thousand coal and iron policemen $2.50 a day. They are furnishing free board and tobacco to these thousands of men and in many cases caring for their families outside the stockade. They are paying five detective agencies that supply most of these men a good weekly commission. In addition to all this, they are under the expense of an office staff that even cut down as it is, compromises fifteen hundred men.
>
> It can thus be easily figured that unproductive labor is costing the operators more than $250,000 each week. This the superintendents do not deny. The other losses can only be guessed at, but the damage done to the mines must be severe and the miners say that several operators are in such a plight that they are seeking terms.
>
> All told it would appear that the operators have incurred an actual money loss of about $2,000,000 since the strike started six weeks ago.[18]

WHAT WILL HE ANSWER?
"Please, can't I have some coal?"
From the *Evening Journal* (New York).

The public's concern about the supply of anthracite, established during the summer months, increased greatly by the time winter approached.
Courtesy of the Ohio State University Department of History.

The special guards hired by the operators were paid high wages, but had little freedom. They soon tired of being cooped up in fortified collieries, living in primitive conditions and being the object of open hostility by most of the local populace:

> The terms of enlistment of many of the special officers who are guarding the mines expired to-day [July 9, 1902] and at The Beaver Brook and Yorktown collieries there were wholesale desertions. The coal companies hereabouts are hiring soldiers returning from the Philippines as colliery guards. These men, the company officials believe, will render excellent service on account of their training and discipline. Many of the guards brought here from the large cities have proven insufficient and their services will be dispensed with.[19]

As July continued, contemporary accounts depicted cracks in the miners' solidarity as an increasing number of strikers returned to work. Despite the pleas of union officials to refrain from violence, striking mine workers continued their previous pattern of personal intimidation toward non-union workers.

> A mob of Silver Brook men captured Rudolph Hensel, a non-unionist workman, last night, and marched him through the mud five miles to McAdoo. Upon arriving in McAdoo the man was paraded through the streets for a half hour at the head of a crowd.
> Then, in a driving rain, he was compelled to kneel at the corner of Blain and Logan streets and pray for fifteen minutes. The man knelt in the mud and carried out the commands of his captors. He was then released and returned to his home.[20]

Despite the growing coal shortages in the cities and the continuing small-scale acts of intimidation and violence, the operators were unable to convince the Commonwealth or Federal authorities to order troops into the anthracite coal regions. However, on July 30 a riot occurred at Shenandoah. A deputy sheriff who was escorting two non-union men into a colliery was attacked by a mob of strikers and was forced to seek refuge in a Reading Railroad depot. The deputy's brother attempted to aid him by smuggling arms into the depot, when he was caught by the mob and beaten to death. The deputy survived and escaped, and the county sheriff contacted Governor Stone, who sent two regiments of the Pennsylvania National Guard into the anthracite regions. Eventually the rest of the Pennsylvania National Guard would be posted throughout the anthracite regions. The Guard's commander, the belligerent General John Gobin, issued orders to his troops to shoot to kill if they were assaulted by strikers.[21]

The arrival of armed troops introduced another variable into an already volatile situation. The removal of the troops became a constant demand by union officials, while some of the guardsmen were themselves members of the working class and thus had empathy with the strikers. Instead of having the calming effect desired by the operators, the stationing of National Guardsmen did not end violence and intimidation, as is shown in the following article:

> Though this region [the Lackawanna Valley] has been a quiet one, the feeling of restlessness among the strikers is beginning to crop out. Hitherto non-union men going to work were not molested. Today an engineer in West Scranton had to draw a revolver to defend himself. When the young men engaged in stoning him saw the weapon drawn they walked off. Trains carrying washery coal are being stoned regularly as they pass through the "Notch," a wild suburb of Scranton.
>
> Last night on the Winton branch of the Lackawanna road an effort was made to dynamite a train of coal. One of the great hog engines was drawing this train. The dynamite shook it up but failed to knock it from the track.[22]

The strikers and their families refused to be intimidated by the stationing of the National Guard. Although they realized that it would be disastrous to directly assault the troops, other ingenious and sometimes humorous ways were found to harass them. This becomes very clear in the *Morning Call*'s description of an incident that occurred at Shenandoah on August 7:

> A crowd of several hundred men made an attack to-day on Company A, Eighth Regiment. The company was encamped on Turkey Run road acting as provost guard. A high bluff overlooks the camp. From this bluff the soldiers were stoned. The guard of ten men went to investigate. As they attempted to ascend the hill, they were met by a shower of rocks and driven back. Then the entire company was aroused and the captain led a bayonet charge up the bluff. The crowd scattered, but turned loose about a hundred dogs. While the soldiers were fighting the dogs several shots were fired at the guardsmen.[23]

Some families were evicted from company housing during the 1902 strike. Courtesy of the Burg Collection, MG-273, Pennsylvania State Archives.

Newspaper reporters often emphasized the melodramatic and poignant aspects of an event such as the Anthracite Strike of 1902. This tendency is termed "human interest." A case in point is the following story, which draws attention to the personal tragedies that resulted from the struggle between strikers and non-union men:

In response to a most pathetic letter calling for aid, General Gobin to-day despatched one platoon of the Governor's Troop to rescue a poor woman and her child, in peril of death from a mob, it proved to be the most adventurous trip yet made by the guardsmen. Upon a winding mountain road the troopers were pelted with stones by men in ambush on the cliffs above, and at two other times the cavalrymen encountered mobs. The letter containing the woman's cry for help was received by General Gobin this morning. This letter reads:

"Turkey Run, August 6.

"To General Gobin, Shenandoah.

"Dear Sir: I now take the opportunity of writing you these few lines to let you know my life stands in danger, and also the life of my husband. We stand in much danger as any one can. The Polanders threaten to blow up my house with dynamite, and they are firing shots around my house every night. I am afraid of my life to lay down to sleep. I call on you for life protection. My bed-room windows were battered in with stones, and my baby was in bed at 2 o'clock in the night, and she was within an inch of her life of being killed. One of the stones lay on the pillow at the side of her head. My child is sick, and so am I.

"They are doing all sorts of planning and plotting in the night time. They are up and down the streets at all hours of the night. Not only that they hung a black and white crape on my door when I got up in the morning I seen it there. Kind sir, please give me some kind of answer, for I am afraid of my life. It would be a blessing if the troops were here for they are needed bad. The reason the foreigner Polanders are down on us so much my husband started to work. He had to, for we had no means of living. We buried a little girl in March and we had not her funeral expenses paid yet when this strike took place. In going down to the outhouse last night a shot was fired at me by a Polander."

General Gobin answered the appeal and sent a detachment of cavalrymen under command of Major Farquahar.

The soldiers found the woman's condition precisely as described in her letter. In their attempts to terrorize the family the strikers had broken every window in the little house. There were marks of hatchets on the doors and many bullet holes in the walls. There was a mob about the house as the soldiers came upon the scene. The rioters retreated sullenly shouting and jeering at the guardsmen.

The besieged woman came to the door with a five-year-old child in her arms. She was crying for joy and tried to kiss the soldiers' hands. Major Farquahar found a carriage and placed the woman and her child in it, escorted her upon an outgoing train. As the soldiers began their return trip they were obliged to stop frequently and by significant gestures toward their carbines dispelled the threatening groups of enraged miners who circled about.

The mob confined its demonstration to curses till the soldiers reached a particularly steep bit of roadway. Then from overhanging cliffs the rioters began hurling rocks on the guardsmen. It was a critical moment, but the officers retained their coolness. Halting the men they made a bluff at preparing for an attack. This sent the rioters scampering from their hiding places and before they recovered from their panic the cavalrymen had passed beyond the danger spot.

Before leaving the hill the cavalrymen stopped at several houses selected at random and in quiet but forceful language gave the citizens in that neighborhood to understand that the frequent attacks upon non-union households must cease.[24]

Despite growing agitation amongst the striking mine workers, the union's officials continued to preach caution and non-violence. However, as operations continued to place the production facilities back in operation, the strikers continued to react forcefully, perhaps instinctively realizing that the successful operation of a number of collieries would give the operators the confidence needed to operate them all. A flash point became the Warnke washery in Luzerne County. The course of this particular confrontation between labor and capital was chronicled almost daily by *Morning Call* reporters. The ultimate result was the inability of the Warnke washery to remain open.[25]

On August 17, 1902, a striker, Patrick Sharpe, was shot and killed by a coal and iron policeman in the Panther Valley town of Nesquehoning.[26] This inspired a series of riots and other acts of violence that wracked this venerable portion of the anthracite fields. As the strike continued, incidents between the coal and iron police and the strikers began to include personal acts of terrorism that will seem all too familiar:

A guard on duty at the Nanticoke colliery was seriously cut on the breast early this morning [August 20]. A striker who had been ordered away from the works agreed to be friendly, and, as the guard took the striker's hand, the latter slashed him with a knife, cutting a severe gash across his breast. Another guard ran to his companion's assistance, and, in his effort to seize the knife, grabbed the blade. Its owner turned the knife suddenly, cutting the guard's fingers so badly that several may have to be amputated.[27]

Besides individual acts of violence, the strikers used public parades to both rally support and persuade the timid not to return to work. Often these processions had almost a carnival atmosphere:

The Dodge colliery of the D. L. and W. Company was the second point attacked by the strikers. There were eighty men at work there and the guards were numerous, so the strikers found it necessary to adopt strategy. Twenty of the workmen were visited at the homes during the night.

By the strikers' method of persuasion, they were made to promise that they would desert and induce their fellow-workmen to do the same. About 200 strikers with a drum corps marched round the colliery. The twenty men started a stampede that was a huge success and within a few minutes there was not a workman left in the place.[28]

A major, if not decisive turning point in the struggle for popular support was the profoundly negative impact of a statement from the Reading Company's president, George Baer. Baer stated in a letter to a Wilkes-Barre clergyman that capitalists had what amounted to a God-given right to manage their property as they saw fit. Quickly dubbed the "Divine Right" speech by the press, it drew shocked and stinging responses from almost all quarters. Among the most eloquent was the following letter which was sent to the newspapers by Father J.J. Curran, a Wilkes-Barre Roman Catholic priest who had consistently support the strikers:

> The many intricate deductions emanating from the sweeping and astounding assertion of Mr. Baer relative to the God-given control of the property interests of the country in the hands of a few Christian monopolists, can be satisfactorily met only by a Socrates or St. Thomas Aquinas. To attempt discussion in a newspaper article of the momentous question raised by the mysterious assumption of the coal operators' salesman would be puerile. If Mr. Baer claims the divine right (God bless the mark!) of ruling his property, he must concede divine right to the miners in working that property. Pharoh, too, must have had the sanction of the gods to rule his land. But Pharoh has been lying at the bottom of the Red Sea for many thousand years.
>
> By way of generalities, I would say this: That the earth is the Lord's, and the fullness thereof. He created it for man's use and benefit. Now if a handful of American millionaires assume divine right to the Lord's earth, where do the people come in?
>
> There should be no more nonsense about the labor difficulties in these coal regions. Let the governor of Pennsylvania call an extra session of the legislature, at the opening of which an investigating committee shall be appointed to get down to the bottom of the trouble and report back at once to the honorable body, and thus settle the question once and for all.[29]

The strike eventually evolved into a contest of perceptions, with the operators attempting in many cases to create the appearance of resuming production, while the strikers did everything in their power to prove that this was not the truth:

> At the Avondale colliery during the night a squad of strikers climbed the stockade to investigate the reports that 100 cars of coal had been brought up from the shaft yesterday. The loaded cars were in plain sight in the yard, but the strikers had their suspicions and tipped over three or four cars. It was found that the mine bosses had filled the cars with dirt and sprinkled coal over the top. The Avondale workmen have been on strike since March, and are getting extra relief from the union.[30]

"HURRY UP AND TAKE THE SMALLER ONE, MR. BAER!"

From the *Record-Herald* (Chicago).

After his "Divine Right" letter, George Baer became a caricature representing the greed of mine owners. The larger cookie in the jar reads "unconditional surrender"; the smaller one reads "arbitration" in this caustic comment on the operators' resistance to arbitrating an end to the strike. Courtesy of the Ohio State University Department of History.

As the strike continued, the gap between union officials, who preached caution, and the initiative of the strikers in maintaining an atmosphere of intimidation became more and more apparent as is shown in the following account of the Klondike Colliery:

A COLLIERY BURNED

HAZLETON, Aug. 27.—The Klondike colliery, owned and operated by Joseph G. Saeger, was destroyed by fire at an early hour this morning.

The Klondike colliery has been operated for the past two weeks in spite of the protests of the union miners. Sager worked the colliery at first under a permit from the United Mine Workers, but a week ago men marched on the plant and drove off the workmen.

The plant was put in operation again yesterday, but a crowd which surrounded No. 10 made a march on the smaller colliery and drove off the workmen.

When the flames were discovered to-day an alarm was sounded, and hundreds of men and boys flocked to the scene. Hardly a hand was raised to stay the destruction of the breaker which was soon totally destroyed. The loss is $8,000. The plant is partially insured.[31]

By September of 1902 the strikers, in spite of relief supplies and money provided to them by the union, were becoming desperate. This desperation was shown by their increasing level of violence against those they perceived to be strike breakers. To the strikers, as long as the collieries remained closed they were winning, and they resorted to deadly force to maintain this condition:

WILKES-BARRE, Sept. 15.—This entire region was in a turmoil this morning, but so far as can be learned only two men were seriously injured as a result of the desperate efforts of the miners to prevent resumption of work. Made angry by the failure of all negotiations in their behalf, the miners covered the anthracite region with pickets at midnight to defeat any attempt of men to return to work.

At Duryea, a small foreign settlement near here, fifty pickets were patrolling the roads this morning. Two Italians were seen in working clothes going along the road toward the Old Forge colliery of the Pennsylvania Coal Company.

"Halt!" yelled one of the pickets. The two Italians instead of halting, started to run.

The picket blew his whistle and gave chase. Within a few minutes fifty men were in pursuit of the fugitives. Most of the pickets are armed with clubs, but a few had revolvers, and seeing that the two workmen were gaining the armed pursuers began to fire.

A bullet struck one of the fleeing men on the back of his head and brought him down unconscious. A moment later two bullets felled his comrade. The fifty or more men composing the mob closed in upon the prostrate men as they lay in front of Toole's Hotel. Almost all the men were foreigners and they kicked and beat the helpless workmen. Then came an alarm that a large force of guards from a nearby colliery was on the way to the rescue and the crowd melted away leaving the two men for dead.

A physician from Duryea was called to their aid and he succeeded in reviving the two men. One of them, as soon as he was able to sit up, put his hand to the back of his head and picked a bullet out of his skull. It had been fired from such a distance that it had just penetrated the skull slightly.

The injured men were able to be helped on a street car in which they were taken to Pittston, where they were met by an ambulance. One of them declined to be taken to a hospital, saying he would rather be cared for at his home. The man with the two bullet wounds was taken to the Pittston hospital where he gave his name as John Gigano. He said he was on his way to work.

At Duryea it is said the injured men were employed as guards at the Old Forge colliery. The sheriff of Lackawanna county and several deputies have gone to the scene of the shooting.[32]

As summer turned to autumn, the level of violence between the strikers and colliery guards increased. *The Allentown Morning Call* continued its daily front-page litany of strike news and some of the reported incidents portray the serious nature of these clashes:

Two riots occurred almost simultaneously in different portions of Pittston this morning and as a result two men were seriously hurt. David Harris, a coal and iron policeman at the Exeter mine, was shot and beaten by three hundred foreigners and will probably die.

William Ahlers, an employe at the Heidelberg mine, was caught by another crowd and clubbed and stoned. Everybody here is praying that troops will be sent as this is the seventh affray in three days.

At the Exeter riot, Felix Rolansky, of Wyoming, and Thomas Thomas, of West Pittston, were both shot during the melee, but neither was seriously injured.

Richard Davis was shot in the leg and John Stroh was beaten over the head with a lead pipe. William O'Hare, a deputy sheriff, was also beaten by the crowd. Superintendent Zorby of the Lehigh Valley Company was early on the scene and stated that troops would be forthcoming within a few hours time.[33]

By the last week of September virtually the entire strength of the Pennsylvania National Guard had been deployed throughout almost all parts of the anthracite region. Many of these soldiers were drawn from the working classes, making them naturally sympathetic to the strikers. Although military discipline was generally well maintained, there were occasional incidents, such as one that occurred in Scranton on September 24, that show that enlisted ranks did not always suppress their inclination to aid the strikers:

Sergeant Malia and Private Brydon, who yesterday assaulted two nonunion men have been court-martialled and were drummed out of camp to-day.

They were stripped of their uniforms and then given a pair of overalls each. As they stepped over the camp line Crippen, a detective of the Delaware, Lackawanna and Western Company, arrested them on a charge of assault and battery and they were taken before Alderman Kasson for a hearing.[34]

Guns, clubs and fists were not the only weapons used by strikers against non-union workers; dynamite now entered their roster of methods of intimidation. An indiscriminate explosive, dynamite could injure an entire family:

At Mahanoy City the home of Michael Weldon, No. 522 West Pine street, was destroyed by dynamite this morning [Sept 29, 1902]. Mrs. Weldon, two children and several neighbors were injured, none of them seriously, however. Weldon is employed as a fire boss at the Schuylkill colliery of the Philadelphia and Reading Company. The dynamite was placed under the front porch of the house and exploded by means of a fuse. The whole front of the house was torn away, and Mrs. Weldon and her children hurled from bed across the room. Glass, wood and stones went flying through adjoining houses, injuring five persons. The lights in the entire city were extinguished, and for a time the residents were terrorized.[35]

As the strike continued, the strikers spontaneously began to plan mass attacks against collieries. Only the intervention of increasingly desperate union officials managed to defuse what could have become pitched battles, as is evident in the following account of events that took place on September 30 at Shamokin:

Troops now hold sway in all five anthracite counties. Colonel O'Neill, of the Fourth Regiment, arrived in Mt. Carmel this morning and selected a campsite for his men, who soon afterward arrived on special trains. One battalion was sent into camp here later in the day. In no portion of the coal fields are troops as welcome to the average citizen as in this county of Northumberland. Sheriff Dietrich delayed making a demand for them till the last possible moment.

Owing to the remote location of Mt. Carmel and the lack of telegraph facilities, not one-tenth of the news of the desperate rioting has been made public. Within twenty-four hours sheriff's deputies have been attacked, bound, gagged, beaten; open assaults have been made by mobs of more than one thousand men upon the Righter, Mt. Carmel, Lehigh Valley and Green Ridge collieries, and machinery has been destroyed in all of these mines. Forty men have been injured. One of them will die. Another is a raving maniac because of his wounds. Two railroad trains have been held up and the cars riddled with bullets and shot.

At midnight an attack in force was planned on the Richards colliery. This mine is defended by thirty guards, a Gatling gun and a searchlight. Throughout the night men assembled in the saloons in the lower part of Mt. Carmel, and as soon as about fifty would get together they proceeded to the outskirts of the town where begins the mountain on which far up could be seen the circling searchlight of the colliery. The sheriff knew all this and was powerless, beyond telephoning brief bulletins of warning to the guards. All his deputies had been dispersed during the afternoon, even those chosen from the ranks of the United Mine Workers at the request of union leaders.

As the hour approached for the attack fully sixteen hundred men, mostly armed with shot guns, lay in the long grass of this mountain discussing the prospect as cheerfully as soldiers going into a regular battle.

They were awaiting the arrival of a tavern-keeper who was to act as leader, when Paul Pulaski, Miles Dougherty, George Hartlein and a dozen other union leaders in this district came running up the road from the Lehigh Valley station. In four or five languages these leaders began impassioned addresses to the men, begging them not to commit the crowning outrage planned.

"We have just been telling the sheriff that if he will recall his order for troops, you will keep peace," cried one leader. That was the first the crowd had heard that troops were coming. At almost the same moment the long-awaited tavern-keeper arrived with a report that the troops were in town and were marching to attack the crowd. This was a false alarm, but it proved effectual, and the sixteen hundred men who had been ready to face armed deputies and to charge in the face of a Gatling gun, began running in all directions upon a rumor of approaching troops.

The breaking up of the big crowd was the signal of the beginning of a series of petty acts of violence. Five or six houses in which non-union men live were stoned; three were almost torn to pieces. The doors and windows were smashed in and the inhabitants were chased and beaten as they fled. In one of these houses the family had been kept prisoners for forty-eight hours by patrols of men who kept watch of the house, waiting to beat the inmates.[36]

It is ironic that not only did the union leadership have difficulties in controlling their men, but the operators appear to have had similar problems as the strike ground on:

Failure to pay them the wages promised, a score of non-union slate pickers at the Reading Company's washery, North Mahanoy colliery struck yesterday. They are nearly all sons of coal and iron deputies.[37]

John Mitchell's strategy of patience and evoking public sympathy for the strikers, coupled with the growing perception that the cities of the northeastern and middle Atlantic region would face a shortage of anthracite for heating, induced President Theodore Roosevelt to intervene. However, the President's actions did not bring about a speedy end to the strike nor did they bring an end to violence in the coal fields:

TAMAQUA, Oct. 9.—With the killing of a striker by an Eighteenth Regiment sentry and the dynamiting of a colliery bridge, the first morning to see the new military force in Schuylkill county began in an exciting manner.

The shooting occurred at Shenandoah. The man killed was William Durham, a mine worker with an excellent reputation. As nearly as the military authorities can learn, Durham was walking quietly to his home early to-day. Near the Reading station he passed a house that had been dynamited a few days ago. Private Wadsworth, of Company A, Eighteenth Regiment, a sentry, one of the newly arrived soldiers from Pittsburg, was on duty in front of the house. He was excited and ordered Durham to halt. Durham either did not understand the order or else did not heed it, for an instant later the sentry fired and Durham fell dead.

The killing has aroused wild indignation among the 18,000 foreigners in Shenandoah. The strike leaders declare it to have been murder and are clamoring for the soldier who did the shooting. He is probably under arrest ...

In the territory under the direct charge of the Philadelphia soldiers, a bridge connected with Slattery's colliery at Tuscarora was destroyed by dynamite last night. A little narrow gauge railroad track passed over the bridge. This enabled the mine cars to reach a chute by means of which railroad cars were loaded. The explosion will retard all shipments for a week or more. ...

Today it became clearly evident that the immediate effect of the ordering of 10,000 soldiers to this region has been to strengthen the strikers' cause. What the later effect will be is not easy to foresee. The mass meetings held throughout the region yesterday as expected, voted unanimously to continue the strike and there is greater enthusiasm in the strikers' ranks than for months past.[38]

By October 15 the negotiations, under the direction of President Roosevelt, appeared to be reaching a successful conclusion, prompting an editorial writer of *The Allentown Morning Call* to compose the following summation. Although displaying the anti-union bias that was found in almost all contemporary newspapers, it does also serve as an unintended testament to the effectiveness of the solidarity that the strikers imposed through use of violence and intimidations:

The present strike was declared by the Mine Workers' Union on the 10th of May, 1902. Since that time many workmen belonging to or not willing to follow that organization were working in and about the mines. From 17,000 to 20,000 [out of a total of approximately 140,000 mine workers] are now at work. Many more have wished to work, but have been prevented by a course of violence and intimidation towards those working and towards their families, accompanied by the destruction of properties and the fear of death or bodily harm to every man who wishes to exercise his right to work.

A schedule is annexed hereto showing some of the things done to create this reign of terror, and every instance stated can be verified by refer-

ence to the officers of the law—civil and military—in the anthracite region. This violence has continued and steadily increased, notwithstanding
repeated disavowals by Mr. Mitchell, and it is clear that he either can not
or will not prevent it, and that the rights of the other workmen can not be
protected under the supremacy of the Mine Workers' Union.[39]

*Michael J. Hoban, Bishop of the Diocese of Scranton, sits between President Roosevelt
and John Mitchell in front of the rectory of Holy Savior Church in Wilkes-Barre, during
the strike. Courtesy of Pennsylvania Anthracite Heritage Museum.*

On October 16, 1902, an agreement brokered by President Roosevelt was
reached between the operators and the United Mine Workers of America. Although the union was not granted formal recognition, the proposed settlement did constitute a great labor victory that could result in a nine-hour work
day, a 10% pay increase, and the establishment of an investigation commission that would take testimony concerning the working conditions in the anthracite fields.[40] On October 20, a convention of the United Mine Workers of
America ratified this agreement. Yet on this same day the intimidation and violence that had so characterized the strike continued in Hazleton:

> Ludwig Meyer, non-unionist, and Arthur Donahue, a mine foreman,
> both of Oneida, were beaten by a mob to-day on their way to Sheppton.
> The mob then marched to the house of Meyer's son and son-in-law, also
> non-unionists, and threatened to blow up the structure.
>   Company E, First Regiment, was called out and dispersed the mob,
> arresting the two ring leaders after a hard chase. The men captured Stan-

ley Yeager and Max Wendel. Yeager is said to have hit Donahue with a club. Donahue is fatally injured. ...

A wedding under the protection of a detail of soldiers at which the bride, the daughter of a non-unionist, and the bridegroom, himself a non-union member, kept a number of the First Regiment members busy yesterday. The wedding in question took place in East Hazleton. Henry Miller, who since the strike has continued working on No. 40 shaft of the Lehigh [Valley] Coal Company, married Daisy Kipler, daughter of another workman.

The guests included a half-dozen or more workmen who refused to come out and their wives and daughters. Just prior to the ceremony Kipler received an intimation that the ceremony was to be prevented by a number of union sympathizers who had declared their intention of stoning the house, which is in a lonely part of town.[41]

The true end of strike conditions can be said to have occurred on October 24, when orders were issued calling for the withdrawal of the Pennsylvania National Guard from the state's anthracite coal region, a troop movement which was completed by the end of the month.[42]

In summary, no historian can deny that it was the combination of conservative leadership of President John Mitchell, his support from members of the business and government communities, his courting of public opinion, and the obstinacy of the operators that were among the foundations for the United Mine Workers of America's victory in the Great Strike of 1902. Yet more than any other factor it was the solidarity of the striking mine workers that brought about this success. Although a significant portion of this solidarity was caused by Mitchell's charismatic leadership, the willingness of the strikers to use intimidation against men willing to work also provided a sense of common cause that held the strikers together, working toward a fixed-purpose victory. If enough men had gone to the collieries, anthracite could have been mined, prepared and shipped to market. Once a significant number of collieries were reopened, the strike would have ended. The striking mine workers instinctively realized this and took a course that was seemingly at a variance with their leaders' orders. In pursuing a course of intimidation and violence they were aided by the belligerence of the special coal and iron police, who were hired from the dross of urban life and were ready to initiate or react to violence at a moment's notice. Although the Great Strike has come to be viewed as a success because of its peaceful nature, it was in reality the use of physical and psychological force by the strikers that kept the mines closed.

Notes

1. The best account of the 1902 strike is Robert J. Cornell, *The Anthracite Coal Strike of 1902* (Washington DC: Catholic University Press, 1957). Mitchell's characterization as a conservative leader is contained in Craig Phelan, *Divided Loyalties: The*

Public and Private Life of Labor Leader John Mitchell (Albany, NY: SUNY Press, 1994), and Perry K. Blatz, *Democratic Miners: Work and Labor Relations in the Anthracite Coal Industry, 1875–1923* (Albany, NY: SUNY Press, 1994).

2.   *The Allentown Morning Call*, 13 May 1902, 1.
3.   Ibid., 24 May 1902, 1.
4.   Ibid., 28 May 1902, 1.
5.   Ibid., 29 May 1902, 1.
6.   Ibid., 4 June 1902, 1.
7.   Ibid.
8.   Ibid. See also Perry Blatz, "The Rebellious Boys of Anthracite: Youthful Labor Protest in the Wyoming Valley," *Proceedings and Collections of the Wyoming Historical and Geological Society,* Vol. XXIV (Wilkes-Barre: WHGS, 1984).
9.   Ibid., 9 June 1902, 1.
10. Ibid., 4 June 1902, 3.
11. Ibid.
12. Ibid., 5 June 1902, 1.
13. Ibid., 11 June 1902, 1.
14. Ibid., 12 June 1902, 1.
15. Ibid., 14 June 1902, 1.
16. Ibid., 18 June 1902, 1.
17. Ibid., 20 June 1902, 1.
18. Ibid., 21 June 1902, 1.
19. Ibid., 9 July 1902, 1.
20. Ibid., 20 July 1902, 1.
21. Donald L. Miller and Richard E. Sharpless, *The Kingdom of Coal* (Philadelphia: University of Pennsylvania Press, 1985; reprint, Easton, PA: Canal History and Technology Press, 1998), 270.
22. *The Allentown Morning Call*, 3 August 1902, 1.
23. Ibid., 8 August 1902, 1.
24. Ibid., 9 August 1902, 1.
25. Ibid., 15-25 August 1902, 1.
26. Ibid., 18 August 1902, 1.
27. Ibid., 21 August 1902, 1.
28. Ibid., 23 August 1902, 1.
29. Ibid., 23 August 1902, 3.
30. Ibid., 28 August 1902, 1.
31. Ibid., 29 August 1902, 1.
32. Ibid., 16 September 1902, 1.
33. Ibid., 25 September 1902, 1.
34. Ibid., 26 September 1902, 1.
35. Ibid., 30 September 1902, 1.
36. Ibid., 1 October 1902, 1.
37. Ibid.
38. Ibid., 10 October 1902, 1.
39. Ibid., 15 October 1902, 1.
40. Cornell, *The Great Anthracite Coal Strike of 1902*, 229–238.
41. *The Allentown Morning Call*, 21 October 1902, 1.
42. Ibid., 30 October 1902, 1.

A sufficient wage to support a family was only one of several issues brought to the fore by the 1902 strike. This miner with his young children is unidentified.
Courtesy of the Pennsylvania Historical and Museum Commission.

The Subcontracting System
and Industrial Conflict
in the Northern Anthracite Coal Field

Robert P. Wolensky

Commissioner Watkins: Would your organization permit a miner to engage three laborers if he could employ them with safety and load ten cars, say?

Mr. [John] Mitchell: No. The organization is opposed to miners employing more than one laborer. The anthracite miners find that the other system [subcontracting system] introduced in this field has done them a great deal of harm. I might say that this matter is entirely local to the anthracite field, and regulated by the anthracite mine workers themselves. It is no well defined policy of the United Mine Workers of America. It is simply a regulation that the miners of the anthracite field find is necessary to protect themselves against favoritism, and against one man going out and hiring a lot of laborers and bringing them in and having them work for him, his being unable to protect them properly against the dangers of mining.

Testimony before the Anthracite Mine Strike Commission, 1902

The tenor of late nineteenth century labor-management relations in the anthracite industry was notably shaped by the operators' insistence on greater control in the workplace, and the workers' desire to improve their economic status and maintain the traditional mining culture. The owners demanded not only lower costs and greater efficiency, but also increased discipline; labor insisted on higher wages and better conditions, and also considerable authority over the work process.

By the 1890s the major coal companies in the northern field around Wilkes-Barre and Scranton had either purchased or leased the mineral rights for the vast majority of coal lands. Through a device called the **subcontract**, a few of the companies—particularly the Pennsylvania Coal Company (PACC) and the Delaware and Hudson Coal Company (D&H)—granted certain individuals a unique temporary access to the coal. The arrangement involved a signed legal agreement between a company and a subcontractor giving the latter the right to act as an independent agent in removing coal in specific seams. Subcontracts were issued for tasks like "robbing the pillars" of coal left from a first mining, and conducting "development work" such as driving main haulage roads (gangways) and main tunnels (headings).[1]

In completing these jobs, the subcontractor typically removed coal in amounts well above the standards acceptable to the collier's traditions and work culture. As such, many workers at the affected companies protested against the subcontracting system. They resented it as an inchoate form of high-output, "factory" mining that had the potential to reorganize the work process, the miners' relationships to each other, and, indeed, their relationship to the coal itself in its legal form as a mineral right.

The Subcontractor Versus the Contract Miner

Unlike the traditional state-certified coal miner, called the **contract miner**, who worked with one or occasionally two laborers at one coal face, the **subcontractor** was usually a certified miner who employed a relatively large team of laborers to load the coal after he had fired it at two, three, or several faces. Carter Goodrich described a similar structure of mining in the bituminous coal industry during the 1890s:

> A more systematic step in the same direction was taken by a number of operators in the nineties who divided the work between groups of "shooters" who were to do the timbering and the shooting and all the skilled work and "loaders" who were merely to shovel the coal.[2]

The subcontractor was not a petty capitalist, because he owned none of the means of production, but he nevertheless functioned as one because of his independence, legal access to the coal, and relatively large work team. Although company haulage men transported his coal to the surface for processing, he was essentially an autonomous operative when it came to removing the raw product. He was paid by the piece (the car of coal) or by the job and, a result of his higher productivity, he enjoyed a much higher income than the contract miner.[3]

The contract miner, on the other hand, had no legal access to the coal but toiled in the single chamber where the company placed him. He was paid by the car of coal or the ton. During the 1890s, approximately 90 percent of the certified miners in the northern and southern fields, and 80 percent in the middle field, worked as contract miners.[4] The balance were either subcontractors or "company miners," the latter employed by the company on projects such as repairing damage and securing the main haulage roads.[5]

Not that certified miners received all of the subcontracts. Testimony given to the Anthracite Strike Commission of 1902–03 indicated that one superintendent at a Lehigh Valley Coal Company colliery "gave a Polish saloon keeper a [sub]contract to rob pillars in preference to his own miners." UMWA President John Mitchell complained to the Strike Commission that "there are instances of saloon keepers taking pillar-robbing contracts and turning them over to practical miners. This means that all the men working on the contract must go to the saloon to be paid, and, of course, leave some of their money on the bar."[6] Even when a bartender or shopkeeper garnered subcontracting rights they nevertheless had to hire a man with "mining papers" in order to conform to the 1889 Pennsylvania law stipulating that only a state-sanctioned person could fulfill the duties associated with the job of miner.

By tradition, the miner hired, fired, and paid his laborers, a practice that the subcontractor continued. In the northern field, the miner usually paid one-third of his gross earnings to the laborer and the subcontractor was presumably bound by that tradition.[7] In the latter part of the nineteenth century, up to 80 percent of the laborers were employed by the day in groups of two to twelve. The balance worked as company men on various above-ground and below-ground projects. Both contract miners and subcontractors usually came from English, Scottish, Welsh or Irish backgrounds while the laborers were usually Slavs, Italians, Lithuanians, or other recent immigrants.[8] The occupational structure reflected the demographic history of the region where Slavs, for example, constituted only two percent of the population in 1880 but 46 percent in 1900.[9]

The Origins of Subcontracting

The policy of contracting the work of miners characterized the British coal industry of the eighteenth century. Coal operators in Northumberland, Durham, the Midlands, and other fields required miners to sign contracts, usually in the spring (the "binding time"), obligating them for 12 months of work. The companies were assured of a stable workforce and miners were guaranteed one year's employment. These so-called contract miners were allowed to hire, train, and pay their laborers. They were remunerated by the piece unit of production, namely, the car of coal, although some were paid by the ton. By custom, the contract miner worked in one chamber at a time with one laborer.[10]

As Pennsylvania anthracite developed in the nineteenth century, operators similarly entered into contracts with individual miners. According to Priscilla Long, "Skilled, or 'practical,' miners were often called contract miners because most of them contracted with the owner to bring out the coal, for which they were paid by the ton, by the yard, or by the wagon."[11] Anthony Wallace characterized the plan as one where "Contract miners were paid by the colliery operator, by the ton or wagon load; they furnished their own tools and supplies; and they supervised and paid their own laborers."[12] One study estimated that, during the first half of the nineteenth century, about one-third of the workforce consisted of contract miners, seven percent were company miners paid by the hour, and the balance were inside and outside laborers as well as other company men who were paid a day rate.[13]

British mining also developed subcontracting schemes. In the eighteenth century, sections of England, Wales, and Ireland initiated the Charter Master System, while Shropshire developed the Butty System. Each were organized around an entrepreneur who, after having secured a contract to mine coal from the mineral-rights-controlling landowner or company, hired miners and laborers to harvest the product. One important difference was that Charter Masters were often not colliers but small businessmen or lessees, while Butties were usually former miners. Workers resisted both plans because of their untoward consequences for autonomy and wages. By the early 1800s subcontracting had virtually disappeared from the northeastern English coal fields, although it persisted in Shropshire until the last quarter of the nineteenth century.[14] Anthracite colliers likewise opposed the subcontract and, as Goodrich noted, "this practice was checked by the increase of the union's [UMWA's] strength" after 1900.[15]

Miners' Freedom and the Subcontracting System

The obligations associated with the traditional contract notwithstanding, nineteenth-century miners viewed themselves as craftsmen and, as such, demanded a full measure of control underground. As certified journeymen, they conceptualized and executed the cutting and blasting, hired and supervised laborers, set production and hours, and took responsibility for safety. In analyzing their well-known ideology of "freedom," Goodrich found that it derived from "the very geography of the working places inside a mine," and from a strong tradition of skilled workmanship.[16] Miners enjoyed great independence because their mine chambers were widely scattered and beyond the immediate control of supervisors. In Schuylkill County in 1870, for example, only 273 bosses supervised nearly 16,000 coal mine workers.[17] Consequently, foremen rarely visited workplaces and the men developed an ethic of independence. They developed workplace values and norms that reinforced a strong occupational identity. Said Long, "It should come as no surprise, therefore, that most [nineteenth-century] coal mines, even quite large ones, represented a proliferation of small underground workshops." [18]

As industrial relations changed in anthracite after the Civil War, the contract also evolved. The companies sought to tighten their command of the workplace such that "the contract itself became the operator's means of control, rather than an agreement between operator and independent miner, presumed equals." [19] After the Long Strike of 1875, for example, coal magnate Charles Parrish of Wilkes-Barre—perhaps the wealthiest "coal baron" in the northern field—"forced strikers from the company homes and refused to rehire them without individual contracts." [20] Parrish preferred a tightly ordered contract with each individual miner rather than a collectively bargained agreement with a union. Over the next half century, conflict raged between the workers and the companies over the matter of individual versus collective contracts.

During the last third of the nineteenth century, miners and laborers organized a series of industrial unions to bolster their occupational position and, at the same time, pursue monetary advantages. The operators vigorously resisted the drive. Three union organizations were established in a 20-year period and the operators defeated each one after an unsuccessful strike: the Workingmen's Benevolent Association (WBA), established in March 1869, fell with the Long Strike of 1875; and the Knights of Labor, active in anthracite since 1871, collapsed with the strike of 1887–88, as did its ally, the Miners' and Laborers' Amalgamated Association, which organized the middle field in 1879.[21]

The United Mine Workers of American (UMWA) became the first association to successfully challenge the operators' dominance. Founded in 1890 from the merger of the Miners' National Trade Assembly 135 of the Knights of Labor, and the Miners' and Laborers' National Progressive Union, the UMWA would take nearly a decade to become a force in anthracite. The new union initiated general strikes in 1894 and 1897, the first ending in defeat but the second bringing modest gains.[22]

For many workers in the northern field, the UMWA was viewed as an ally in the fight against the subcontracting system, which they had been resisting for several reasons. The first was a concern for equal opportunity and its obverse, favoritism. The men complained that the policy encouraged preferential treatment because subcontracts were issued to more agreeable (i.e., anti-union) or otherwise favored miners (i.e., through ethnicity, religion, politics, etc.), or to those willing to pay kickbacks—a type of graft that was outlawed by the Pennsylvania General Assembly in 1897. They were also issued for more attractive seams that offered "easy" coal, and subcontractors were treated more favorably in the distribution of empty coal cars.

Safety was the second concern. Because a subcontractor worked two, three, or more places simultaneously, he could not easily follow state laws requiring that only certified miners fire a charge, prop the roof, and erect timbers. Alterations in wages and work culture constituted the third complaint. If subcontracting were to spread, said the critics, the companies would need fewer contract miners, forcing many to become laborers in order to make a living. The program would weaken the craft heritage, de-skill the workforce, and diminish wages.[23] It could also divide the highest ranking craft—certified miners—by placing one small element in a position superior to the great majority, and weaken their overall occupational status.

The coal companies, on the other hand, favored subcontracting for various reasons. Some workers possessed superior physical and mental attributes, they argued, and should be encouraged to win greater tonnage.[24] Moreover, as owners or lessees of mineral rights, the companies insisted on their legal claim to grant any type of contract to any individual without interference from government or organized labor. The operators also realized direct economic advantages through the scheme because subcontractors could more deliberately command and "push" their hirelings toward greater productivity and output.[25]

The companies most likely preferred the subcontract for another reason: it could serve as an effective weapon in the growing conflict with organized labor. Subcontractors in various other industries such as garment manufacturing, iron molding, stone quarrying, and railroad-locomotive manufacturing found ways to bypass wage standards, production quotas, and work rules. As David Montgomery noted, "Subcontracting practices readily undermined both stints [worker-induced production quotas] and the mutualistic ethic [among workers] ... and they tended to flood many trades with trained, or semi-trained, workers who undercut wages and work standards."[26] Consequently, if the scheme proved effective in controlling a rebellious work force while lowering costs and boosting productivity, it could also help bolster anthracite's faltering competitiveness.

The Competitiveness Problem in Anthracite

Toward the end of the nineteenth century, the competitive advantages enjoyed by the bituminous industry were apparent. While the harvests of anthracite and bituminous remained fairly even until the Civil War, thereafter bituminous took the lead. By 1900, soft coal constituted 80 percent of all U.S. coal production. The contrast in the relative *values* of the fuels showed an equally distressing trend. In 1880, anthracite's output was worth $42 million while that of bituminous was put at $53 million; by 1890 the figures were $66 million and $110 million respectively; and in 1900, $85.8 million and $221 million.[27]

The increasing cost of doing business also hindered the anthracite producers. Frank Warne found that mining increased 31 cents per ton between 1880 and 1890, while the value of the coal at the mine increased only 11 cents per ton.[28] Although soft coal could not replace hard coal in all markets, especially in anthracite's main market of home heating, the omens for the future in manufacturing and steam generation were disconcerting.

The coal industry as a whole lagged well behind other industries in implementing modern technological and production efficiencies. In comparing the contemporary factory with the typical coal mine, Goodrich found a wide difference:

> The *indiscipline* of the mines is far out of line with the new *discipline* of the modern factories; the miner's freedom from supervision is at the opposite extreme from the carefully ordered and regimented work of the modern machine-feeder. The contrast is sharp and striking, and moreover it is not merely a static one.[29]

As the anthracite corporations realized their increasingly disadvantaged situation, several constraints shaped their response. Geology presented a crucial geological limitation. Unlike the soft-coal companies, the anthracite operators could not overcome the resource-depletion problem by discovering more accessible deposits in other regions. Because anthracite was found only in northeastern Pennsylvania, they were forced to dig deeper and more costly shafts that accessed ever-thinning seams.[30]

Capital investment represented an important financial constraint. Despite consistently high rates of return, the operators were often reluctant to make investments in new plants and equipment. For example, while the bituminous industry matched improvements in cutting technologies with advances in drilling and blasting, anthracite saw few such parallels. The percussive puncher used in bituminous at the end of the nineteenth century was replaced by a chain-breast machine early in the new century, to be followed by short-wall machines around 1910. Anthracite rarely utilized these innovations, although blasting and drilling technologies did advance.[31]

Even with an oligopoly established by the J.P. Morgan railroads by 1902, over-production remained another persistent problem for hard coal. The first organized effort to constrain tonnage and manipulate supply occurred in the southern field in the early 1850s. Later in that decade, northern producers joined their southern counterparts in a short-lived restriction plan that fell victim to the panic of 1857.[32] In 1868, numerous small operators agreed to reduce tonnage by supporting a WBA-sponsored work stoppage associated with the Pennsylvania eight-hour work law.[33] In 1873, the coal-carrying railroads instituted the first successful combination to stabilize supply and prices, although it lasted only a few years. They reformulated similar agreements five more times before 1900.[34] In 1898, the highly consolidated industry established a production plan through a so-called "community of interest" among the mine-owning railroads. These "coal pools" actually had the opposite of their intended effect and instead stimulated over-building and over-production because the allocation quotas were based upon each operator's output capacities.[35]

Another reason for over-production, pointed out by G.O. Virtue in 1896, was that the mining of ever-deeper and more-expensive measures forced the companies to recover their investments through greater yields.[36] Moreover, as David Brody noted, the "market characteristics of coal set it apart from other sectors of heavy industry." He pointed out that the demand for anthracite remained "inelastic," meaning that price increases did not significantly affect demand, at least in the short run, because consumers needed the coal. Supply, on the other hand, was "elastic" when demand increased, meaning that production readily expanded due to the ease of entry into the business, but "inelastic" as demand fell because many operators, especially independents, would take low or even no profits rather than cut output or shut down.[37]

A final constraint facing anthracite was the labor problem. Relations between workers and operators had been among the most rancorous of any American industry. The operators were willing to spend any amount or go to any length to keep the unions out and the individual contract in, so as to maintain control over their facilities. Labor, on the other hand, remained profoundly aggrieved regarding specific company policies such as low pay, excessive "docking" for coal waste, conflict over the height of the "topping" on coal cars, and the subcontract. Within these acrimonious relationships, the subcontracting scheme emerged as one of several workers' complaints in the strike calls issued by the UMWA in 1900 and 1902.

The Strike of 1900

By 1900, the coal corporations controlled by Morgan's five railroad lines—Philadelphia & Reading, Lehigh Valley, Jersey Central, Lackawanna, and Erie—were producing nearly 62 percent of the anthracite. When the shipments contracted from independently owned companies were added, the so-called Line companies commanded over 80 percent of the market. They not only dominated access to the mineral reserves but transported approximately 60 percent of the product in 1901.[38]

As labor-management conflict expanded through the 1890s, numerous strikes hit the anthracite region including actions at Lattimer in 1897, and at Duryea, Pittston, and Nanticoke in 1899.[39] The hostility peaked with a union-initiated shutdown that began on September 17, 1900, and continued for 47 days. Although the UMWA had an official membership of only 8,000, over 100,000 mineworkers from all three anthracite districts (No. 1 in the northern field; No. 7 in the middle field; and No. 9 in the southern field) backed the boycott.

The strike of 1900 involved three issues: wage rates, policies, and work organization. Unlike all previous anthracite strikes (excepting 1887–88), which were organized to prevent a reduction in wages, the action in 1900 called for a pay increase. The men also demanded changes in company policies that indirectly lowered earnings, such as the sliding scale (used in the southern and middle fields), high blasting powder and company store prices, excessive dockage, and the 3,360 pound (as opposed to the 2,240 pound) ton that applied to miners paid by weight.

In anticipation of the impending labor-management talks, union representatives from the three anthracite districts met in Hazleton on August 27, 1900, and drafted nine demands. The *third* of the nine provisions spoke to the subcontract. It insisted on "no more than one breast, gangway or working place for one miner at any time nor more than an equal share of cars and work for any miner." [40] The statement addressed the "hoggish" reputation of the subcontractor as well as his preferential treatment in securing better workplaces and empty coal cars. It also signaled a warning that the mineworkers opposed the reorganization of work that the subcontract implied. Subcontracting, therefore, emerged as the workers' main *non-wage* grievance.

Despite dissatisfaction with the practice, subcontracting did not rank among the UMWA's top priorities as the bargaining unfolded. This was clear when President Mitchell sent an envoy, Daniel J. Keefe, president of the International Longshoremen's Association, for pre-strike negations with the operator's chief mediator, Senator Mark Hanna. In this exchange, Mitchell insisted that five issues would have to be addressed in order to avoid a shutdown: reduction in the price of powder to $1.50 per keg, abolition of company stores, abolition of the sliding scale, modification of the dockage system, and a pay increase of at least 10 percent.[41]

The UMWA removed the subcontract issue from the list of demands for two probable reasons. First, because the system existed at only a few firms, it was not yet a widespread practice. Second, the UMWA's precarious status in the negotiations, coupled with its conservative leadership, led to a focus on the economic position of the members. Challenging what was essentially a property right—a company's ability to issue contracts for mineral rights that it owned or controlled— would be far too radical a proposal that would have to wait for a later time.

The companies initially refused to bargain any of the issues and, indeed, argued that market conditions actually required a wage cut. Because of an impending national election, however, the operators yielded to political pressure applied especially by Hanna, who was also chairman of the Republican National Committee.[42] The strategy apparently helped William McKinley win the presidency with Theodore Roosevelt as vice president. The mineworkers also realized an important victory that included a 10 percent wage increase and some other concessions. It was their first significant strike-related triumph in more than 50 years of conflict with the companies. For decades, anthracite workingmen celebrated the October 29th return-to-work day as "Johnny Mitchell Day."[43] Despite the historic success, several issues remained unresolved, including the matter of the subcontract.

The strike of 1900 marked a watershed in anthracite industrial relations for another reason. If previously the operators could bolster sagging profits by directly lowering wages through rate cuts, or indirectly lessening them through larger coal cars, higher powder prices, increased company store prices, and greater dockage, with the newfound power of the UMWA the old methods would no longer apply. In order to remain competitive—which included a pattern of very high returns to stockholders—the companies would have to realize new technological, managerial, or organizational efficiencies. As Warne counseled in 1901, "If there is any one thing certain as to the future of the anthracite coal industry it is that the cost of mining must be reduced more and more."[44]

The Strike of 1902

Although most observers considered the strike of 1900 a triumph for the UMWA, the unsolved issues led to over 100 wildcat strikes during the following year.[45] Industrial tensions culminated in the union-authorized strike of 1902, "the most important single event in the history of American trade unionism until that time. ..." [46]

The conflict pitted an emerging union power of 125,000 members against an established industrial giant with a capitalization approaching $200 million.[47] The walkout began on May 15, 1902, and continued for 163 days. The strike represented the first time in American labor history when "a labor organization tied up for months a strategic industry ... without being condemned as a revolutionary menace." [48] The issues that had precipitated the strike of 1900 remained. Although the mineworkers had several grievances, the UMWA submitted four demands for the final negotiations. The first called for a 20 percent increase in wages; the second, a 20 percent reduction in work hours; the third, payment by the ton; and the fourth, recognition of the UMWA and the establishment of a grievance procedure.[49] The last demand was accompanied by an argument critical of the subcontract, which was described as an individual or a special agreement that referred to the subcontract:

> The anthracite mine workers should not be compelled to make or sign individual agreements but should have the right to form such organization and choose such agents and officers as they desire to act collectively instead of individually whenever they deem that their best interests are subserved thereby.[50]

On the other side, the companies were resolute on no wage increases, the same hours, per-car payments, and no UMWA legitimacy. They also wanted to boost productivity well beyond the rate of two or three cars per man, while the colliers sought to maintain or even lower the production level that they hoped would raise prices and wages.[51] In April 1902, at the initial pre-strike meeting between the operators and the union leaders, the Erie Railroad president, Eben Thomas, articulated the operators' three basic positions. The first was that there would be no consideration of the closed shop, while the third insisted on no standardized wage in anthracite because of the variability between mines and working conditions. The second proposition addressed the question of production and, by implication, the subcontract:

> That there shall be no deterioration in the quantity or quality of work, and that there shall be no effort to restrict the individual exertions of men who, working by the ton or car, may for reasons satisfactory to themselves and their employers produce such a quantity of work as they may desire.[52]

The subcontract, therefore, remained a contested issue before, during, and after the strike. When the three anthracite union districts met in a pre-strike convention in Shamokin in March 1902, delegates from locals at PACC collieries submitted a resolution against the practice, which was approved by the delegates:

> *Whereas*, The [sub]contract system which some of our men are subject to at present and which an effort is being made by the companies to put in force in several of their collieries under a large scale, which is detrimental to our organization. And *Whereas*, Those working for said [sub]contractors are violating the laws of our Union in every respect ... And *Whereas*, This system of work has caused more men to become traitors to our organization than any other system of work ever introduced into our coal fields, and subject our men who remain faithful to us by being cut short in their cars to supply [sub]contractors on days when the collieries are idle. And *Whereas*, The Erie Coal Company are the foremost in having this system put in force as through this system they can have their coal mined thirty per cent. less by giving it out to [sub]contractors who will make at least thirty per cent. on each man who works for him. ...
>
> *Resolved*: That this convention takes into consideration the danger of this [sub]contract system *especially under the Erie Coal Co.*, and force said company to give up said system of work and have our men work at the same, as it was worked before the contract system was introduced. And be it further Resolved, That we the employees of the Erie Co., ask this convention to stand by us in whatever stand we may take to abolish this contract system.[53]

Another resolution that was approved also expressed opposition:

> Whereas, it is a well-known fact that in many sections of the anthracite region there is a system of [sub]contract in vogue which is, and has been very obnoxious and vicious in its fulfillment. Inasmuch that in many cases one man employs from four to twenty laborers, and in some cases the [sub]contractor seldom enters or comes near the work for one or two weeks at a time, and this in itself is not the cause of principle advocated by the U.M.W. of A.; therefore, be it resolved that any member of the organization who shall contract for such work as will necessitate the employment of more than two laborers, excepting such contracts as shaft sinking, slope sinking or tunnel driving, shall be expelled from the U.M.W. of A.; and we, the members of the U.M.W. of A., absolutely refuse to work with any man so expelled from the union.[54]

Some UMWA locals imposed severe penalties on members who accepted subcontracts, as in the case of PACC employee William Zarn, a miner from Dunmore, who

> ... told of having been compelled [by the union local] to give up a [sub]contract at a big loss. ... This was in February, 1901. He took a

[sub]contract to rob pillars and employed thirteen men. The union protested and summoned him to come to a meeting of the Local. He told the Local he had lost money on the [sub]contract and asked to be given a little more time, that he might recoup some of his losses. The Local voted to let him take out ten cars a day for two months. Three days later, the driver boy gave him only six cars, and when asked why he was not getting ten, [he was] told that the president of the Local instructed him to deliver him only six cars.[55]

At the Delaware and Hudson Coal Company, much of the strife surrounding the subcontract involved the so-called heading men, who dug new openings. In November 1901, the company entered into agreements with several heading men at the Jermyn Colliery near Scranton. Their removing large amounts of coal brought a storm of protest from UMWA members. According to a summary of the testimony of Thomas R. Thomas, an inside foreman at colliery, before the Strike Commission:

> The company was desirous of pushing the "heading" work to open up a large new territory. The heading men also were willing and anxious to push the work. The union sought to prevent them from doing any more than was being done by the "chamber men" [contract miners] and took various means of enforcing its ideas. First, the boys refused to give the heading more than "their share" of cars; that is, more than the chamber men were allowed. On Dec. 13, 1901, the company discharged two drivers who refused to give the heading men cars that were sent to them. Other boys, who refused to take the places of those discharged, were also discharged. The whole work force went out on strike, but after a few days agreed to come back if the boys were all reinstated. The company agreed to reinstate them, if they would do as they were directed.
>
> The Local instructed the boys to obey orders and work was resumed. At the same meeting, it was afterwards learned, a resolution was passed reading as follows: "Unless all heading men cease loading more than their share of cars you will be expelled from the union."
>
> On the Saturday night following the meeting, some party or parties entered the mine and destroyed tools belonging to three of the heading men: Michael McHale, Harry Gilbert and Henry Richards, who had disregarded the notice.[56]

Some of the driver boys continued to deliver empty cars to the heading men but several laborers refused to load the coal. When company officials were convinced that the union was forcing the laborers' actions, they closed the Jermyn Colliery on December 31, 1901. Following two weeks of negotiations, they reopened the facility after receiving assurance from the union that no further "molestation" of the heading men would occur. However, when heading man John Sobey refused to limit production, his home was sabotaged by dynamite.[57]

Heading man Michael McHale, who had worked at the colliery for seven years, appealed to the UMWA for a special dispensation. McHale contacted the district organizer, Henry Collins, to make his plea whereupon he was referred to District 1 president, Thomas D. Nicholls. But after a brief meeting, Nicholls agreed to the importance of McHale's work and allowed him to continue. After a short time, co-workers leveled another complaint against the subcontractor.

> McHale attended a meeting of his Local and explained the terms and conditions of his [sub]contract. In spite of this the Local decided that he could not load any more cars than the men who were working in breasts and chambers got [i.e., the contract miners]. Again the matter went to Nicholls, who, this time, said that he could do nothing for McHale, the Local must handle it. The Local then decided that McHale must lay off two of the nine laborers working for him and he finally did so. Soon afterward someone smashed $10 worth of his tools one night.[58]

Another heading man, Harry Gilbert, alternatively worked day and night shifts. During the day he loaded the same number of cars as the contract miners, which was two per man, but at night he usually sent out nine cars. In October 1901,

> the drivers and runners told him that the Local had ordered them not to give him cars at night unless Gilbert would agree not to load more cars than day men did. The company wanted the place completed quickly. The trouble was not settled and in December Gilbert was suspended by the Local "until such time as he will live up to the rules." [59]

It is clear from the testimony before the Strike Commission that workers at most northern collieries adamantly insisted on producing two or three cars (depending upon the size of the car, which varied from company to company and even colliery to colliery). The operators, for their part, wanted a greater yield and saw the quotas as a defiant act. Company executives decried the "spirit of insubordination" among the men, particularly since the 1900 strike. PACC's district superintendent, Henry McMillan, told the Strike Commission that his workers disregarded his entreaties to produce "that extra car of coal" to help the company:

> Witness told that, in 1901, one of the shafts at the Barnum Colliery was thrown idle. He asked the men at the other shaft to load a little extra coal to help out the company. They refused to do so, saying they had an agreement to send out not more than "eight hours" of coal. The witness explained that this means coal enough to supply the breaker for eight hours." [60]

Victor L. Peterson, general superintendent of the Hillside Coal and Iron Company, cited the case of UMWA member Richard Holland, who "loaded ten cars [per shift] prior to 1900, and who now can not be induced to load

Henry Demarest Lloyd (left), John Mitchell (center) and Clarence Darrow during the strike of 1902. Demarest, an outspoken critic of the owners of big businesses, was to die the following year.

more than six." When asked what reason men like Holland gave for the change, Peterson answered, "They simply say, 'that's enough.'" "Can they load more?" asked the chairman of the Strike Commission. "They have loaded more," replied Peterson.[61] Theodore Hogan, a foreman at PACC's Avoca Colliery complained that before the strike of 1900, his men were sending out three cars per shift working alone, and five cars in pairs; however, "soon after the close of the strike the men began to diminish their output." He threatened to take disciplinary steps to compel greater output, but the District No. 1 president, John T. Dempsey, warned of labor action so Hogan relented.[62] In this particular case, the company had to hire 50 extra employees in order to attain the desired yield. In was apparent, therefore, that the organized militancy against increased production presented a challenge to both the authority as well as the profit margins of the companies. The subcontracting issue became enmeshed in a broader conflict over output which was, at root, a contest over workplace control.

Statistical reports indicated that output had indeed fallen about one car per shift after 1900. At one Lehigh and Wilkes-Barre Coal Company operation, the union local was alleged to have passed a resolution limiting production to six cars for a three-man crew, when previously they had loaded seven to fourteen. Production cutbacks were documented at Delaware, Lackawanna & Western Coal Company, the Lehigh and Wilkes-Barre Coal Company, D&H, and PACC.[63] The workers' resistance to greater output continued after the 1902 strike. Statistics showed a slight decline in daily output from 2.27 tons per man between 1893 and 1902, to 2.23 tons between 1902 and 1912.[64]

For the mineworkers, workplace control was not the only controversy underlying the subcontract. Fairness and work equity stood as paramount considerations. When management cited cases of contract miners and laborers producing below capacity, the union replied that workers were more concerned with fairness in distributing work. UMWA chief attorney Clarence Darrow articulated the union's view before the Strike Commission:

> The Chairman [Judge George Gray]: I understand, Mr. Darrow, that you take issue of the general statement and charge here that there is any restriction on the output of the miner placed upon him by the union.
>
> Mr. Darrow: Why, to be sure.
>
> The Chairman: I just wanted you to know. You do take that position?
>
> Mr. Darrow: Yes. I do not deny but what the miners have sought to regulate the crusts that have been thrown to them so that one man should not have a loaf while the other has nothing. But they have not done it because there are too many [empty coal] cars. If those men were furnished the wark [sic] and the cars according to their own statements, there will be no restrictions anywhere in this region. Let them take their own writ-

ten records furnished to this commission and see the story they tell. I do contend, and I always shall, unless I change my mind—and I have studied these questions a good deal—that where there is not work enough to go round, common justice and common rumanity [sic] would say that one man should not jump in and eat all there is and leave the rest hungry, and that is all the miners have attempted to do in this case.

The Chairman: Enough to go around where? The whole community?

Mr. Darrow: To those miners whom they carry on their payrolls. If they do not want them, let them discharge them. So long as they carry them, they are employes [sic] of the company, and it is right that there should be regulation and some fair equality amongst them men, when there is not enough to go around. That is our position in that matter.[65]

On October 23, the parties agreed to arbitration under the 7-member Anthracite Coal Strike Commission appointed by President Theodore Roosevelt. The Strike Commission's final ruling granted a ten-percent wage increase and a reduction in work hours from ten to nine hours. It also established the Anthracite Board of Conciliation to adjudicate future grievances. The union had emerged as a force to be reckoned with, although the settlement did not address many consequential issues. The subcontracting controversy did not go away following the settlement; indeed, it remained a intensely debated issue over the next three decades.

The Persistence and Evolution of the Subcontracting System

The UMWA called for an end to the subcontract in every labor-management negotiation between 1902 and 1923. These included 1906, 1909, 1912, 1916, 1920, and 1922. For example, in 1906, the union's first demand was "that no contract miner shall have more than one working place at the same time," nor "more than two laborers at the same time." The operators continued to resist the idea, arguing that

We have no such legal or moral right to establish such arbitrary rules. Men must be free to act for themselves. Where the conditions are such as to safely permit men to work we cannot consent to limiting the ability and ambition of industrious men by arbitrarily agreeing to restrict their opportunities to earn increased remuneration.[66]

Montgomery noted that the subcontract was a source of persistent conflict in the decades following the 1902 strike, "until large numbers of Italians, enrolled in the IWW, fought for the suppression of the [sub]contract system in 1916."[67] The IWW (Industrial Workers of the World) began organizing anthracite in 1906, and the effort came to a climax with a strike against PACC in 1916. Subcontracting figured significantly into the shutdown according to organizer Arturo Calvini, who told reporters, "the contract system of the Pennsylvania Coal Company caused the unrest."[68] When the strike failed—keeping PACC the field's only non-union company—the defeated IWW left the hard coal fields.[69] The subcontracting system continued at the PACC, Hillside, and D&H companies into the late 1920s. Major revolts over the scheme occurred at PACC collieries in 1920 and 1928, with numerous small conflicts in between. Following the 1920 strike, over 10,000 PACC workers joined the UMWA for the first time.[70]

In preparation for the 1916 negotiations, UMWA delegates protested against a group of subcontractors who were excavating as many as 30 chambers at one time.[71] When the 1916 talks were settled and the UMWA had, for the first time, gained partial legitimacy as the bargaining agent, some union leaders believed the new agreement would end subcontracting. UMWA president John B. White optimistically stated that "this form of recognition … destroyed the subcontractor with his Padrone system."[72] As events later revealed, his sanguinity was unfounded.

White's "Padrone" reference was to the bonded-contract labor system used in Sicily's sulfur mines and elsewhere in labor contracting.[73] During the 1910s, PACC employed a large number of Sicilian subcontractors who hired their countrymen as laborers in a manner reminiscent of the exploitative old-world arrangement. Indeed, references to the Padrone system in anthracite date at least to the mid-1890s. For example, although Italians did not constitute a large share of the mining work force, Terrance Powderly, former president of the Knights of Labor and mayor of Scranton, testified in 1895 that "The 'Padrone' system does exist in every large and small center, and particularly in the mining regions." [74] PACC's Sicilian employees protested against the subcontracting system at least partly because they associated it with an "old country" injustice.

During the negotiations of 1920, the UMWA again demanded "That the making of individual contracts in the mining of coal be prohibited." When an impasse resulted another federal commission, this one appointed by President Woodrow Wilson, settled the debate. The Anthracite Coal Commission of 1920 granted a 17-percent wage increase and gave further legitimacy to the UMWA. Rank-and-file mineworkers did not approve of many of the commission's terms, however, so they walked out on an 18-day "vacation strike." Under threats from the President himself, they soon returned to their jobs.[75] One of the contested issues was the commission's refusal to terminate the subcontract. Neal J. Ferry, the mineworkers' representative on the body, wrote a minority report that, while admitting to a company's right to engage in contracts, asked the commission to "declare in favor of collective bargaining as a general principle and against individual contracts that tend to supersede or substitute for the basic award or agreement." Neal also wanted the commission to allow subcontracts only in "isolated cases" due to "abnormal [mining] conditions." [76]

The first demand submitted by the UMWA for the 1922 talks again asserted that "the making of individual agreements and contracts in the mining of coal shall be prohibited. ..."[77] The stalemate that year led to a protracted strike of 163 days that was arbitrated by another federally appointed body, the United States Coal Commission of 1922. This commission gave the subcontract much more attention than had previous inquisitions. In its final report, the commission ruled that a corporation's right to issue contracts was firmly embedded in the nation's laws. It cited cases such as Lochner v. New York (1905), where the U.S. Supreme Court struck down a law limiting the workday to 10 hours on grounds that the measure infringed on a company's freedom to contract within the meaning of the due-process clause of the fourteenth amendment.[78]

Recognizing the intractability of the subcontracting policy, the UMWA took a different tack for the 1923 negotiations. The union demanded that subcontractors conform to all standard wage rates and work rules. Management agreed and both sides approved a clause requiring that "no contracts shall be made with individual employees at less than the prescribed scale rates or not in keeping with customary practices."[79]

Because of the 1923 agreement, the UMWA did not mention the subcontracting issue in the talks of 1925. The inability to resolve differences that year led to anthracite's longest strike, 170 days. After a short hiatus, the plea to abolish subcontracting reappeared on the union's demand list in the 1930s, 1940s, and early 1950s. A partial achievement was realized in the 1936 negotiations when the operators agreed to the UMWA's request that all subcontractors sign the union agreement.[80] In 1939, representatives of Districts 1, 7, and 9 joined with their management counterparts to pass a joint resolution abolishing subcontracting: "RESOLVED, that special and individual contracts in the mining of coal where now in use shall be eliminated."[81] Because the resolution was not binding or enforceable, it was ignored.

At last, with the 1952 agreement the five-decade-old problem of the subcontract was eliminated in District 1. According to an official union statement:

> It is with a great deal of satisfaction that your officers inform you that they have succeeded in abolishing the system of special or individual contracts in District No. 1. The long sought goal of the Union was attained only after years of unrelenting efforts. As far back as 1920, an anthracite commission appointed by President Woodrow Wilson declined to eliminate the system. ... Hardly a convention or a joint conference passed, however, without the UMWA renewing its fight against the system which had such a baneful effect on our contractual structure. ...
>
> The death knell of the system was sounded in the 1952 Agreement with the incorporation of a section in which the signatories agreed to the elimination of special and individual contracts within thirty (30) days after November 16, 1952, the effective date of the pact. ...[82]

The former Butler Colliery of the Pennsylvania Coal Company in Pittston Township was leased to the Volpe Coal Company in the 1930s. Courtesy, Stephen N. Lukasik

The goal that had occupied three generations of anthracite workers came as a hollow victory, however, as the news had to be tempered by the fact that the large companies had instituted a new method organizing mineral-rights access, the **leasing system**. Beginning in the 1930s, the large companies began systematically leasing large sections of mines and eventually entire collieries to relatively small incorporated firms often headed by former subcontractors or mine supervisors. Lessees were usually required to sell all of their coal to the lessor, who processed and sold the final product. Many other lessees processed their own coal but had to pay a royalty to the lessor plus a fixed annual amount. PACC and the Lehigh Valley Coal Company had leased virtually all of their collieries and coal properties by the late 1940s, and the field's three other major producers—Glen Alden, Hudson, and Susquehanna—were moving in the same direction.[83] Some of the leaseholding firms such as the Volpe Coal Company, the Kehoe-Burge Coal Company, the Jermyn Greene Coal Company, and Pagnotti coal interests grew to become some of the larger producers of anthracite.

Although opposition to the subcontract was regularly part of the UMWA's bargaining demands, President John L. Lewis did not make it a priority in his negotiations with the companies. He finally spoke against the leasing system at the Tri-District Convention of March 1939, held in New York City:

> Some of the great coal companies have followed the practices of leasing out their coal lands and their collieries to individuals and companies of doubtful responsibility. They have failed to include as a stipulation in those leases that those lessees should be responsible to the degree that

they will pay the rates under the industry, and as a result the chaos has been intensified and large operating companies have found themselves in the unique and paradoxical position that they have been unable to compete in the open market, with the lessee mining coal upon their own property and paying them a royalty for the right to mine.[84]

UMWA vice president Thomas Kennedy also denounced the scheme's negative influence on the "payment of wages and the maintenance of working conditions, [and] the stabilizing of the price." He said that "most companies in the anthracite industry" engaged in leasing and concluded that the arrangement "has done more to bring about instability and chaos in the industry than anything else I know of." [85]

Ewen Colliery of the Pennsylvania Coal Company, Port Griffith, leased to the Pittston Coal Company in 1929. Courtesy, Frank Hizny.

Miners and laborers who had worked for the old Line companies, the subcontractors, and the new lessee firms viewed anthracite's tenancy schemes as devices to lower wages, divide the workforce, and weaken if not destroy the UMWA. According to Knox Coal Company laborer William Hastie, "In order to break the union, or to weaken it, they installed that contracting system." Another laborer, John Usefara, who worked for Morgan Bird in the 1950s, a lessee from the Glen Alden Coal Company, agreed:

"They did the leases to get rid of the union." Charles Adonizio, whose father and uncle began as subcontractors for the Pennsylvania Coal Company in the 1920s, believed that the big companies initiated tenancy agreements because "… they wanted to get away from the union … [which] started to come in there strong in the '20s." From management's side, Alex Chamberlain, whose family had been in the coal business since the mid-nineteenth century, concurred: "It was a way of companies insulating themselves from labor." [86]

Both the subcontracting and leasing systems became riddled with corruption. Bogus inspections, short weights, illegal mining, and wage- and work-rule violations became common. The UMWA eventually became part of the dishonesty. It was a corrupt leaseholding firm, the Knox Coal Company, that mined illegally under the Susquehanna River near Pittston in 1959 and caused an inundation that ended deep mining in the middle portion of the northern field and facilitated the demise of the anthracite industry in the Wyoming Valley area. The Knox Company, which had leased coal holdings from PACC beginning in the 1943, was partly (and secretly) owned by District 1 president, August J. Lippi.[87]

Summary and Conclusion

After Carter Goodrich had surveyed the mining occupation from the 1890s to the 1920s, focusing particularly on the bituminous industry, he predicted that modern administrative methods such as Scientific Management, as well as mining devices like high-speed cutters, would diminish the miners' renowned independence and bring a new order of efficiency and discipline to the industry. However, the anthracite industry was not the bituminous industry. Goodrich's predictions notwithstanding, modern management and mechanization were not the forces that transformed the anthracite industry and its workplace culture in the northern field. Rather, a combination of factors related to anthracite's competitive position resulted in the spread of the subcontracting and leasing structures, which, in turn, reorganized access to mineral rights and "tamed" the labor force. With the tacit approval of the large mining corporations, the contractors and lessees invoked a strict disciplinary canon that took direct aim at the miners and laborers, their work culture, and the union. Productivity and control became the bywords. The large companies engaged the services of subcontractors and lessees precisely because they were more effective in subduing labor, reorganizing work, and maintaining competitiveness. As the last president of the Penn Anthracite Collieries Company in Scranton recalled: "These people [subcontractors and lessees] could do what we couldn't do. … They could do things that the company wouldn't, couldn't do … such as get the extra car of coal from the men which often meant the difference between profit or no profit." [88]

Of course, the industry's broader economic crisis facilitated the companies' actions. The fall-off in demand following the 1925–26 strike, coupled with the national economic decline after the stock market crash of October 1929, saw the number of mining operations drop from 163 to 113 between 1929 and 1932.[89] Employment plummeted 39 percent during the period 1927–1933, from 167,648 to 102,469 workers.[90] As thousands of jobs were eliminated workers responded with calls for *equalization,* or the equitable distribution of available work among all workingmen within a company.[91]

Although workers resisted the subcontracting structure at the grass-roots level, the UMWA organization, including President John L. Lewis, were ill-equipped and unwilling to directly challenge companies. The national organization's recalcitrance helped precipitate the formation of a short-lived dual union in the northern field, the United Anthracite Miners of Pennsylvania, in 1933, which garnered thousands of members and paralyzed the industry with strikes between 1933 and 1935. Equalization and an end to the subcontract were two of the most important policies fostered by the new union.[92]

The UMWA missed important opportunities to address the tenancy issue during the strikes of 1900 and 1902, and during subsequent negotiations (and strikes) over the next 30 years. Conservative union leadership and its neophyte status can perhaps explain the union's lack of fervent opposition during the 1900 and 1902 negotiations. On the other hand, John Mitchell and his colleagues most likely realized that American labor law was no match for American corporate and property law, especially when reinforced by the political and ideological influence of the coal corporations. Because John L. Lewis, who ruled the UMWA for 40 years, emphasized productivity, mechanization, and business unionism, and rarely challenged policies related to the organization of work, overcoming the subcontract and the lease remained a low priority. Nevertheless, the protest against the tenancy structures continued at the grass roots for a half century. By the time subcontracting was eliminated in District 1 in 1952, the leasing system, with its many corruptions, was in full force and the northern field's deep-mining industry was in its last years.

Notes

1. The testimony of numerous company officials and mineworkers at the 1902 Anthracite Strike Commission hearings indicated that these particular companies were the main users of the subcontract. Likewise, Anna Rochester confirmed that "Contract miners of this petty boss type are employed only by certain companies in the northern part of the anthracite region." See Anna Rochester, *Labor and Coal* (New York: International Publishers, 1931), 129. Why these companies implemented the subcontracting system is a topic beyond the purpose of the present study.

2. Carter Goodrich, *The Miner's Freedom: A Study of the Working Life in a Changing Industry* (New York: Arno Press, 1977 [1925]), 130.

3. Rochester (*Labor and Coal,* 129) pointed out that, despite their small numbers,

subcontractors pulled up the average wage of the larger group of miners in statistical reports.

4. Frank J. Warne, "The Anthracite Coal Strike," *Annals of the American Academy of Political and Social Science* 17 (1901): 33.

5. No records on the number or percentage of subcontractors have been found, although period and subsequent literature suggests very small numbers, perhaps no more than two or three percent.

6. *Proceedings of the Anthracite Mine Strike Commission, 1902–03*, published by the Scranton Tribune, 146.

7. Warne ("The Anthracite Coal Strike," 32) discussed the one-third pay figure for laborers. No evidence was found regarding the subcontractors' reneging on this custom.

8. David Montgomery, *The Fall of the House of Labor: The Workplace, the State, and American Labor Activism, 1865-1925* (New York: Cambridge University Press, 1987), 334. However, see note 71 below regarding the changing ethnicity of the subcontractors.

9. Victor R. Greene, "A Study in Slavs, Strikes, and Unions: The Anthracite Strike of 1897," *Pennsylvania History* 31 (1964): 200.

10. T.S. Ashton and Joseph Sykes, *The Coal Industry of the Eighteenth Century* (Manchester, England: Manchester University Press, 1929 [1964]), chapters 6 & 7.

11. Priscilla Long, *Where the Sun Never Shines: A History of America's Bloody Coal Industry* (New York: Paragon House, 1989), 59.

12. Anthony F.C. Wallace, *St. Clair: A Nineteenth-Century Coal Town's Experience With a Disaster-Prone Industry* (New York: Alfred A Knopf, 1987), 133.

13. Clifton K. Yearley, Jr., provided this workforce profile of a typical southern field mine employing 100 men in 1850. See his *Enterprise and Anthracite: Economics and Democracy in Schuylkill County, 1820–1875* (Baltimore, MD: Johns Hopkins University Press, 1961), 170.

14. On the Butty System see A.J. Taylor, "The Sub-Contract System in the British Coal Industry," in L.S. Pressnell, ed., *Studies in the Industrial Revolution* (London: University of London–The Athlone Press, 1960), 214–35; and Dave Douglass, "The Durham Pitman," in Raphael Samuel, ed., *Miners, Quarrymen and Saltworkers* (London: Routledge & Kegan Paul, 1977), 226–36. On the Chartermaster System see Ashton and Sykes, *Coal Industry*, 100, and Michael W. Flinn and David Stoker, *The History of the British Coal Industry*, Vol 2 (Oxford, England: Clarendon Press, 1984), 55–56 & 377.

15. Goodrich, *The Miner's Freedom*, 130.

16. Ibid., 17.

17. Long, *Where the Sun Never Shines*, 60.

18. Ibid., 65.

19. Ibid., 64.

20. Victor R. Greene, *The Slavic Community on Strike: Immigrant Labor in Pennsylvania Anthracite* (South Bend, IN: University of Notre Dame Press, 1968), 68.

21. Harold W. Aurand, *From the Molly Maguires to the United Mineworkers: The Social Ecology of an Industrial Union, 1869-1897* (Philadelphia: Temple University Press, 1971); Greene, *The Slavic Community on Strike*, Chapter 4.

22. On the founding of the UMWA see Selig Perlman, "Upheaval and Reorganization (Since 1876)," Part 4, Vol 2, in John R. Commons et al., *History of Labour in the United States* (New York: Macmillan, 1918), 487; and Maier Fox, *United We Stand: A History of the United Mine Workers of America, 1890-1990* (Washington, DC: United Mine Workers of America, 1990), Chapter 3.

23. *Proceedings of the Anthracite Mine Strike Commission*, 17.

24. Ibid.

25. See Goodrich, *The Miner's Freedom*, on the conflicts between management and labor over mechanization and traditional mining practices.

26. David Montgomery, *Workers' Control in America: Studies in the History of Work, Technology, and Labor Struggles* (New York: Cambridge University Press, 1979), 12–15.

27. U.S. Geological Survey, *Mineral Resources of the United States, 1910*, Part II—Non-metals (Washington, DC: USGPO, 1911), 22. The trends were similar with regard to petroleum, although that fuel's advantage came later, as hard coal's historically higher value had vanished by World War I. In 1920 the fuels' comparative values were $434 million for anthracite and 1.36 billion for oil. By 1925 figures showed an even greater unevenness: $328 million versus $1.29 billion respectively. See U.S. Bureau of the Census, *Historical Statistics of the United States: Colonial Times to 1970* (Washington, DC: USGPO, 1975), 590–93 (coal production statistics); 582–83 (coal value statistics); 582 (petroleum value statistics). Although the value of natural gas increased throughout the first half of the twentieth century and certainly helped erode anthracite markets, the total value of the fuel would not exceed anthracite's until the 1950s (ibid., 582, natural gas value statistics).

28. Warne, "The Anthracite Coal Strike," 41.

29. Goodrich, *The Miner's Freedom*, 13–14. Original emphasis.

30. For data on the digging of deeper and thinner coal seams, see Harold Barger and Sam H. Schurr, *The Mining Industries, 1899-1939: A Study in Output, Employment and Productivity* (New York: National Bureau of Economic Research, Inc., 1944), 184.

31. Anthracite's inadequate investment in plants and machinery continued throughout the first half of the twentieth century. Two of hard coal's larger corporations illustrated the pattern. Between 1922 and 1931, the Glen Alden Coal Company yielded an average annual return on stock of 144 percent. The Lehigh and Wilkes-Barre Coal Company realized a 100 percent stock dividend in 1924, and over 44 percent per year between 1909 and 1929. When the companies merged in 1929 to form anthracite's largest producer, total debt amounted to just over $52 million. By the end of 1940, the debt had been reduced to about $34 million and by 1951 to less than $1 million. Meanwhile, after-tax earnings between 1931 and 1951 amounted to $79 million, the great bulk of which was disbursed to stockholders. Meanwhile, the investment in fixed assets amounted to only $17 million between 1931 and 1951. As one consultant concluded in the 1950s: "It is apparent that the policy pursued was one of reduction of debt and payment of dividends, with only a small reinvestment to improve properties." As a consequence, wrote the consultant, "present facilities are largely obsolete and in some instances poorly maintained. Even small labor-saving devices have not been purchased and put to use." See Paul Wier Company, "Report on Operations of Glen Alden Coal Company, July 1952," as cited in Robert A. Janosov, "Glen Alden's Huber Breaker: 'A Marvel of Mechanism,'" in *Canal History and Technology Proceedings* Vol 11 (Easton, PA: Canal History and Technology Press, 1992), 133.

32. Yearley, *Enterprise and Anthracite*, 158–64.

33. Marvin W. Schlegel, "The Workingmen's Benevolent Association: First Union of Anthracite Miners," *Pennsylvania History* 10 (1943): 244.

34. Eliot Jones, *The Anthracite Coal Combination in the United States* (Cambridge: Harvard University Press, 1914), Chapter 3 & Appendix, Table 6. The cartel-like efforts by coal companies to manipulate supply and price was not limited to the U.S. In Britain the operators formed The Grand Allies which, from 1710 to 1726, worked "for the purpose of restricting output and raising the price. As such it has much in common with other associations of owners, though for a time it was more successful than most." See Flinn and Stoker, *History of the British Coal Industry*, 40.

35. The nineteenth century consortiums failed, said Long (*Where the Sun Never Shines*, 123), because "When prices started rising [the companies] scrambled to produce more than their agreed-upon allotment. The system was constantly breaking down." Warne ("The Anthracite Coal Strike," 21) discussed the demise of the 1898 consortium: "Among the operators it is known as 'an understanding among gentlemen. ...' [but] the statistics of production show that the collieries rarely, if ever, keep within the allotments."

36. G.O. Virtue, "The Anthracite Combinations," *Quarterly Journal of Economics* 10 (April 1896): 296–323.

37. David Brody, "Market Unionism in America: The Case of Coal," In *Labor's Cause* (NY: Oxford University Press, 1993), 132.

38. Jones, *The Anthracite Coal Combination in the United States*, 103–106. See also Scott Nearing, *Anthracite: An Instance of Natural Resource Monopoly* (Freeport, NY: Books for Libraries Press, 1915), chapter 7; Warne, "The Anthracite Coal Strike," 18.

39. Perry Blatz, "Local Leadership and Local Militancy: The Nanticoke Strike of 1899 and the Roots of Unionization in the Northern Anthracite Fields," *Pennsylvania History* 58 (1991): 278–97; Greene, *The Slavic Community on Strike*, 156–60.

40. *Minutes of the Twelfth Annual Convention of the United Mine Workers of America* (Indianapolis: The Hollenback Press, 1901), 29. The other eight demands were: (1) an advance of twenty percent on all day labor receiving less than $1.50 per day, fifteen percent on all classes of day labor receiving between $1.50 and $1.75 per day, and ten percent on all day labor receiving more than $1.75 per day; (2) abandonment of the sliding scale system in practice in the middle and southern regions; (4) abolishment of the 3,360-pound ton, 2,240 pounds to constitute a ton; (5) employment by the miners of a checkweighman to see that the weight registered is correct and dockage fair; (6) reduction in the price of powder to $1.50 per keg; (7) abolishment of the company-store system; (8) abolishment of the company-doctor system with compulsory payments; (9) compliance with the State law providing for semi-monthly pay in cash. On the demands see Warne, "The Anthracite Coal Strike," 29.

41. Robert Cornell, *The Anthracite Coal Strike of 1902* (Washington, DC: The Catholic University Press, 1957), 54.

42. Robert H. Wiebe, "The Anthracite Strike of 1902: A Record of Confusion," *Mississippi Valley Historical Review* 48 (1961): 229–51.

43. The mineworkers actually received an *average* 10 percent increase that varied among the companies. Moreover, as a later coal commission pointed out, "The [pay] advance took the form of a reduction in the price of [blasting] powder and an increase in the wages paid." (See U.S. Coal Commission, *General Report* (Washington, DC: USGPO, 1923), 330.) Furthermore, the increase was directed at contract miners working underground, not their laborers. As the laborers in the northern field received one-third of the miner's gross earnings, their wages would be expected to rise proportionately.

44. Warne, "The Anthracite Coal Strike," 51.

45. *Proceedings of the Anthracite Mine Strike Commission*, 25, 97–98. On the labor unrest following the 1902 strike see also Joe Gowaski, "John Mitchell and the Anthracite Mine Workers: Leadership Conservatism and Rank-and-File Militancy," *Labor History* 27 (1985): 54–83.

46. Selig Perlman, *A History of Trade Unionism in the United States* (New York: Macmillan, 1923 & 1937), 177.

47. There were approximately 100,000 men and 50,000 boys working in anthracite, but because the boys were counted as one-half members, the total potential membership amounted to 125,000. Warne ("The Anthracite Coal Strike," 16) put the capitalization figure at $161,784,473 in 1890.

48. Perlman, *Trade Unionism*, 177. Importantly, according to Perlman, "What distinguished the anthracite coal strike ... was that for the first time a labor organization tied up for months a strategic industry and caused wide suffering and discomfort to the public without being condemned as a revolutionary menace to the existing social order calling for suppression by the government; it was, on the contrary, adjudged a force within the preserves of orderly society and entitled to public sympathy."

49. Anthracite Coal Strike Commission, *Report to the President on the Anthracite Coal Strike*, March 18, 1903, 40–42.

50. Ibid., 42.

51. A tradition dating back to at least the 1890s called for two or three cars per person per shift. (See *Proceedings of the Anthracite Mine Strike Commission*, 146.) Montgomery (*Workers' Control in America*, 13) found that workers in various industries engaged in "rationally restricted output" because the practice reflected "unselfish brotherhood," "personal dignity," and "cultivation of the mind." It also prevented "hoggish behavior" and other forms of individualism and "anarchic competition" while supporting mutuality among workers.

52. Quoted in Cornell, *Anthracite Coal Strike*, 83.

53. *Proceedings of the Tri-District Convention 1902*, 20–21. The Erie Railroad controlled two anthracite companies at this time, the Pennsylvania Coal Company and the Hillside Coal and Iron Company.

54. *Proceedings of the Anthracite Mine Strike Commission*, 14.

55. Ibid., 146.

56. Ibid., 131–32.

57. Ibid.

58. Ibid., 132.

59. Ibid., 132.

60. Ibid., 145.

61. Ibid., 145.

62. Ibid., 146.

63. General testimony regarding the production cutbacks appeared in ibid. 84 & 156. Production cutbacks at specific companies were listed in ibid. as follows: the Delaware, Lackawanna & Western Coal Company (p. 157); the Delaware & Hudson Coal Company (p. 133); Pennsylvania Coal Company (p. 146); and the Lehigh and Wilkes-Barre Coal Company (p. 170).

64. U.S. Coal Commission, *Report on 1923 Strike* (Washington, DC: USGPO, 1925), 331.

65. *Proceedings of the Anthracite Mine Strike Commission*, 168.

66. *The Anthracite Coal Controversy, Demands of 1906*, uncatalogued information sheets, Anthracite Heritage Museum, PHMC, Scranton.

67. Montgomery, *The Fall of the House of Labor*, 334.

68. On the IWW strike see "Sheriff Will Prevent All Meetings of I.W.W.," in James Bussacco, *Pittston's Coal Mining Era* (compilation of original newspaper articles and images published by the author, 1995), 196; "Police Gather In Saloon Assembly," ibid., 194; "500 Laborers Are Driven From Region By The I.W.W. Strike," ibid., 191.

69. Patrick M. Lynch, *Pennsylvania Anthracite: A Forgotten IWW Venture, 1906–1916*, M.A. thesis, Bloomsburg State College, 1974.

70. Perry K. Blatz, *Democratic Miners: Work and Labor Relations in the Anthracite Coal Industry, 1875–1925* (Albany, NY: SUNY Press, 1994), 240–250; Douglas K. Monroe, *A Decade of Turmoil: John L. Lewis and the Anthracite Miners, 1926–1936*, Ph.D. diss., Georgetown University, 1976, 81–92.

71. Although PACC employed many Sicilian subcontractors, as Selig Perlman discovered in his investigations for the Commission on Industrial Relations, the ethnic dimensions of the system had changed at other companies by this time: "The [sub]contractor is more often a Pole than he is an English-speaking person. The [sub]contractor gets as many cars as he needs and the bona fide contract miner is often short of cars. Very frequently the [sub]contractor runs a saloon or boarding house and is not a miner himself." Quoted in Montgomery, *The Fall of the House of Labor*, 334.

72. *Proceedings of Tri-District Convention 1916*, 70.

73. On Sicily's sulfur mines see Eric J. Hobsbawm, *Primitive Rebels: Studies in Archaic Forms of Social Movement in the 19th and 20th Centuries* (New York: W.W. Norton, 1959), 5, 36, 41, 45. On the larger prevalence of labor contracting in the late nine-

teenth and early twentieth centuries see Gunther Peck, "Reinventing Free Labor: Immigrant Padrones and Contract Labor in North American, 1885–1925," *Journal of American History* 83 (1996): 848–71.

74. Quoted in Herman Stump, J.H. Senner, and Edward F. McSweeney, *Report of the Immigration Investigation Commission to the Honorable Secretary of the Treasury* (Washington, DC: USGPO, 1895), 36. Oral history evidence has suggested that bonded laborers arrived in the northern anthracite field from Sicily during the early twentieth century. See William Hastie, taped interview, 31 July 1989, Northeastern Pennsylvania Oral History Project (hereafter NPOHP), tape 2, side 2.

75. On the vacation strike see Blatz, *Democratic Miners*, 245–47.

76. Neal J. Ferry, "Minority Report," *Report, Findings, and Award of the Anthracite Coal Commission of 1920* (Washington, DC: USGPO, 1920), 312–323. The quotes are from p. 321.

77. "The Miners' Demands," *The Anthracite Strike of 1922* (Philadelphia: The Anthracite Bureau of Information, 1923), 5.

78. Samuel P. Hays, *The Response to Industrialism, 1885–1924* (Chicago: University of Chicago Press, 1959), 159.

79. *Award of the Anthracite Coal Strike Commission, Subsequent Agreements, and Resolutions of the Board of Conciliation* (Hazleton, PA: Anthracite Board of Conciliation, 1923), 47.

80. *Proceedings of Tri-District Convention 1935)*, 75–77; Monroe, *A Decade of Turmoil*, chapter 8.

81. *Award of the Anthracite Coal Strike Commission, Subsequent Agreements and Resolutions of Board of Conciliation* (Hazleton, PA: Anthracite Board of Conciliation, 1 July 1953), 182.

82. *Proceedings of District No. 1 Convention 1957*, 19.

83. We discuss this development of the contracting and leasing systems at PACC and other companies in Robert P. Wolensky, Kenneth C. Wolensky, and Nicole H. Wolensky, *Mineral Rights, Tenancy Agreements, and Labor Conflict: The Contracting and Leasing Systems in the Northern Anthracite Industry*, unpublished manuscript.

84. *Proceedings of Tri-District Convention 1939*, 7.

85. Ibid., 12.

86. William Hastie, taped oral history interview, 31 July 1989, NPOHP, tape 2, side 1; John Usefara, taped oral history interview, 28 July 2001, NPOHP, tape 2, side 1; Charles Adonizio, taped oral history interview, 14 March 1996, NPOHP, tape 1, side 2; Alex Chamberlain, taped oral history interview, 11 July 1995, NPOHP, tape 1, side 2.

87. Robert P. Wolensky, Kenneth C. Wolensky, and Nicole H. Wolensky, *The Knox Mine Disaster: The Final Years of the Northern Anthracite Industry and the Effort to Rebuild a Regional Economy* (Harrisburg, PA: Pennsylvania Historical and Museum Commission), 1999.

88. William Graham, taped oral history interview, 11 July 1995, NPOHP, tape 1, side 2.

89. Monroe, *A Decade of Turmoil*, 28.

90. Pennsylvania Department of Mines and Mineral Industries, *Annual Report: Anthracite Division*, 1962, 10.

91. John Bodnar, *Anthracite People: Families, Unions and Work, 1900–1940* (Harrisburg, PA: Pennsylvania Historical and Museum Commission, 1983), 1–17. See also Thomas Dublin, "The Equalization of Work: An Alternative Vision of Industrial Capitalism in the Anthracite Region of Pennsylvania in the 1930s," *Canal History and Technology Proceedings* Vol 13 (Easton, PA: Canal History and Technology Press, 1994), 81–98.

92. On the United Anthracite Miners of Pennsylvania, see Monroe, *A Decade of Turmoil*, 242–320.

The headquarters of the Pennsylvania Coal Company in Dunmore.
Courtesy of National Canal Museum.

Disturbance of the Peace:
The Operators' View of the
1902 Anthracite Coal Strike

Richard G. Healey

The need of the hour is for the keen moral insight of capitalists and entre-preneurs to be exercised so that they will deal justly by labor. [1]

With these quaint if not slightly patronizing words, Peter Roberts, in his classic study of the anthracite industry, sought to exhort the financiers and coal operators of the day. He urged them to utilize their refined moral sensibilities to bring justice in their dealings with the common working man, whose "defective education" needed to be supplemented by discipline and supervision. While such sentiments would hardly be deemed acceptable in a present-day text on labor relations, this very fact is a caution to us about the implicit application of contemporary standards to past times and places. Stereotypical "coal barons" and "robber barons"[2] are easy targets for caricature, rebuke and criticism and they were often their own worst enemies, in terms of the public image they presented through the media of the time. Nevertheless, there is a need for a modest re-appraisal of their stance in the 1902 strike, in part because of the availability of new evidence. Such a study should focus on their specific world-view and it will act as a useful counterpoint to earlier studies that have effectively pressed the case from the labor perspective.[3]

No attempt will be made here to provide a chronological treatment of the activities of the operators before and during the strike, or of their conferences with representatives of the United Mineworkers of America (UMWA) and the National Civic Federation (NCF). This can be found in Cornell's admirable and comprehensive study.[4] Instead, the operators' stance will be examined under three main headings. The first of these relates to the underlying principles, which the operators claimed guided their actions. The second is the nature of their detailed approach to the strike and negotiations with union representatives and other intermediaries. Thirdly, an assessment needs to be made of the UMWA view of the way in which the operators ran the coal business, with particular reference to the scale and distribution of profits derived therefrom. Prior to a detailed consideration of these issues, a brief overview of the structure of the industry at the beginning of the twentieth century will be given, by way of background.

Background to the Structure of the Industry

The anthracite coalfields were commonly divided into three "regions": the Wyoming, Lehigh, and Schuylkill regions. The first of these corresponded to the Northern coalfield, the second to the Eastern Middle Field and the eastern tip of the Southern Field. The remainder of the Southern Field and the Western Middle Field constituted the Schuylkill region. Until the beginning of the 1870s, the Schuylkill and Lehigh regions were the province of small individual coal operators, who shipped their product to market over the common carriers of the Philadelphia and Reading Railroad and the Lehigh Valley Railroad.[5] In the Wyoming region, transportation companies with mining privileges, such as the Delaware Lackawanna and Western RR (DL&W) and the Delaware and Hudson (D&H), assumed major importance from a very early stage, but there were also a significant number of independent coal operators.[6] During the 1870s, by means of subsidiary coal companies, the Philadelphia and Reading, the Lehigh Valley and the Central Railroad of New Jersey all acquired substantial coal estates. That of the Philadelphia and Reading was by far the largest, comprising over 100,000 acres, which gave it effective control over much of the Southern and Western Middle fields.[7] The Pennsylvania Railroad also acquired a controlling interest in a number of smaller mining and transportation companies concentrated at the western end of the Schuylkill and Wyoming regions.[8] In later years the Erie Railroad extended its control over hard coal traffic by taking over both the New York, Susquehanna and Western Railroad and the Pennsylvania Coal Company. The New York, Ontario and Western Railroad acquired the former coal properties of companies such as the Lackawanna Iron and Steel Company and the Elk Hill Coal and Iron Company in the Scranton area.[9]

By 1901 John Mitchell, President of the UMWA, asserted that 90% of all anthracite coal was owned by seven of the major railroads, whereas prior to the 1900 strike the figure had only been 75%. He also predicted that within a short time railroads financed by J.P. Morgan would own "absolutely all anthracite coal."[10] Similar observations can be found in Roberts' study, written at the same time.[11] However, it would be wrong to imagine that the arrival of the UMWA precipitated sudden and major changes in the structure of the anthracite industry. Mitchell and Roberts are in fact only describing what might be termed the "endgame" in a much longer process of progressively increasing control by the major transportation companies. In the very early period, independent mine operators were essential business partners of the corporations. This was because the latter did not have sufficient mining capacity to meet market demand at all seasons of the year or to keep their own railroads and gravity railroads in full and economic operation.[12] After the Civil War, when the railroads first actively engaged in combination to restrict coal supply and hold up prices,[13] the tonnage of independent operators tributary to the lines of the major railroads was crucial in the maintenance of percentage tonnage allocations between the different interests. To prevent independent operators changing allegiance between railroads, assuming their property was actually or potentially accessible to more than one line, they were bound into a variety of long-term tonnage contracts. These required them to ship defined and large quantities of coal via the specified railroads, spread over a period of years. Failure to abide by the terms of the contract could result in the mine being taken over and operated by the railroad's mining subsidiary. The only circumstance feared by the railroads was bankruptcy by an independent operator, since this would result in abrogation of the contract, generally followed by a sheriff's sale of assets and the possibility of the mine being acquired by a competing interest.[14]

A distinction also needs to be maintained between ownership of coal lands and conduct of mining operations. Some of the railroads' coal subsidiary companies, such as the Philadelphia and Reading Coal and Iron Company (PRCIC) and the Lehigh Valley Coal Co. (LVCC), had a policy of leasing portions of their coal lands to individual operators as tenants. In 1901, for example, 22% of the shipments of the LVCC were made by tenant operators.[15] Taking account of these tenants, calculations made by the Anthracite Coal Operators Association indicate that as late as 1890, 42% of anthracite was mined by individual operators. By 1900 the percentage had declined to 29.7%. It fell still further, to only 17% the next year,[16] following the trend to absorption by the railroads that Mitchell and Roberts identified. The key point, however, is that the individual operators continued to have a significant role in the daily conduct of the anthracite business until the beginning of the drive for unionization in the coalfields by the UMWA at the turn of the century. In this context it is also important to note Mitchell's observation in 1901 that the experience of the UMWA had been that the coal subsidiaries of the railroads were "much more reasonable than the individual or independent operators. However this is accounted for by the fact that the individual or independent operators are absolutely at the mercy of the railroads."[17] This assessment of the balance of economic power is open to a measure of dispute, because of the appetite of the railroads for coal tonnage, but the differing degrees of truculence noted by the UMWA need to be highlighted. There were other important differences between the individual and the railroad subsidiary operators, as we may term them. These related particularly to such matters as employment contracts, attitudes to discharge and the company store. Since the larger independent operators, such as the Pardees, Coxes and Markles in the Eastern Middle Field,[18] tended also to be geographically concentrated, this had an impact on the attitudes of labor to the operators in different parts of the coal regions. These issues will be examined in more detail in the ensuing sections.

The Underlying Principles of the Operators

Given the differences between types of operator and their relative importance in the marketplace, it is perhaps unwise to assume too great a uniformity in their views on the anthracite industry and labor relations within it. Nevertheless, Berthoff has argued that the labor policy of the railroad subsidiary operators, at least, was the product of a "genuine spirit of autocratic benevolence—a device on the part of the owner to protect his own view of the common interest in which he felt his employees should share." [19] General statements of this kind, however, conceal a range of issues that need to be examined more closely, before the overall perspective of the operators can be assessed.

In particular, it appears that a number of underlying principles guided the approach of the operators to the conduct of their business. None of them are specific to the circumstances of the 1902 strike, but all were called into play during the period in question. This period is taken to include the pre-strike discussions and the Coal Strike Commission Hearings, as well as the strike itself. These principles can be enumerated as follows:

- The importance of management control of the business
- The rule of Law
- The right to work

The importance of management control of the business

The easy caricature of all-powerful capital which tyrannizes the downtrodden laboring masses is not particularly helpful in understanding the operators' perspective on this issue. [20] Instead, there are several different aspects that need to be considered quite specifically. The first of these concerns property rights in general, and the unwillingness to cede control to outside labor organizations, in particular. Secondly, there is the genuine legal responsibility to manage companies in the interests of shareholders, a matter that has been largely overlooked in previous studies. Finally, there is the complex question of operating, overtly or covertly, within the constraints of a cartel or combination.

It was doubtless the legal background of G.F. Baer, president of both the Reading Railroad and its subsidiary coal and iron company, that led him to his specific focus on the question of property rights and management control. His view was most succinctly put in his well-known lecture entitled "Work is Worship," delivered at Franklin and Marshall College on January 16, 1902. In this lecture he argued that "the owner of property has a right to control its lawful use" and that without such control ownership was "a mere sham and delusion." [21] In Baer's mind, such ownership implied, of necessity, that no element of control could be ceded to any outside organization that had no rights in the business and therefore no means of enforcing any dictates relating to it. As he stated to John Mitchell in his letter of 18 February 1902, "there cannot be two masters in the management of business." [22] However, it is important to note that this stance in relation to labor organizations had a very long history in the anthracite coal business and Baer was simply the latest in a long line of operators to restate it. For example, during the 1877 labor troubles in the Lehigh region, Ario Pardee, as spokesman for the independent operators, declared "our position always has been, and is now, that we are unwilling to negotiate with anyone outside our employ, who knows nothing of our business and who is in no way connected with us." [23] Pardee restated this view when testifying during the investigation into labor troubles in the anthracite regions in 1887–88, adding in relation to the Knights of Labor, "I have been on [sic] a chronic fight with these organizations. I commenced it in 1847." [24] Leaders of labor organizations were well aware of the depth of feeling by the operators on this question and had marshaled their arguments against it. This is apparent from correspondence contained in the Coxe Family Mining Papers, which have recently become accessible to scholars. During the labor troubles of 1887–88, W.T. Lewis, Master Workman of the Knights of Labor, wrote to Eckley B. Coxe as follows:

> The objection that you will consult with none but your employees, if there is such an objection on your part, is hardly tenable even from a technical standpoint, as the great volume of the world's business is done by and through agents. It would be impossible for any human being to transact your enormous business, hence you have delegated it to agents. So it is with miners, what business they cannot transact they delegate to those whom they think can do it for them.[25]

Unfortunately, Eckley Coxe's reply, if indeed one was made, has not been traced. Although arguments such as these have some logical force, it is clear that they made no impression on the settled views of the operators.

The avowedly oppositional stance of both individual and railroad subsidiary operators to what they perceived as meddling in their affairs by external organizations did little to foster good employee relations. Yet in the case of the railroad subsidiary operators, at least, there was equally some legal force to their particular stance. As Baer observed in another of his well-known quotes, "the Laws organizing the Companies I represent in express terms impose the business management on the President and the Directors. I could not if I would delegate this business management to even so highly a respectable body as the Civic Federation." [26] Although quoted in Cornell,[27] no emphasis is placed in the latter study on the quite genuine responsibilities of corporate managers and directors to fulfil their legal obligations and act in the interest of their bondholders and shareholders. A further quotation from Baer's correspondence (also noted by Blatz[28]) makes this clear:

I never was so determined in my life. I can afford to stand a strike and the losses that will result therefrom; but I cannot afford, with my eyes open, voluntarily to bankrupt my Company by inviting losses that any man charged with the responsibility of management would say were unnecessary and unwise.[29]

Since this was written privately to other railroad presidents, his "Co-partners in patience" as the letter is headed, it is reasonable to assume this genuinely reflected his views, rather than being simply his negotiating stance towards the UMWA.

Limitations of space preclude further development of this topic here. However, a case can be made that the operators should be judged by history a little more in terms of the constraints and obligations under which they worked, and a little less in terms of the clumsiness of their handling of public relations during the strike. The specific question of their financial constraints will be addressed in more detail below.

The final issue under the heading of management control of the business is the complex matter of operating within the confines of the anthracite coal combination, which was established in 1873. Detailed chronologies of events surrounding the formation, dissolution and re-establishment of the combination can be found in Schlegel[30] and Jones,[31] so only its significance for corporate management needs to be considered here.

Over the years a variety of devices for restricting production were employed by the cartel, including periodic suspensions of mining, regular but restricted working, e.g. three days per week, or restriction in the supply of cars to the mines. Clearly these methods required the operators to be in complete control both of coal supply and transportation facilities, to enable them to act in concert. Extended strikes deprived the operators of control over coal supply, so their mines could not work on days when, according to the cartel, they should have been engaged in production. This brought with it the risk of loss of market share, as any shortfall in their own tonnage would readily be made up by other companies. Actual percentages of the total output in previous years were used in negotiations for tonnage allotments in subsequent years, so unexpected declines in shipments could have adverse consequences in the longer term also.[32]

At the beginning of 1872, prior to the establishment of the cartel, the Reading Railroad, for example, had reported with favor on the apparent willingness of the Workingmen's Benevolent Association to "agree with their employers upon a fair basis of wages for the ensuing season."[33] However, they also noted that the combined effect of strikes and fluctuations in the coal trade had directed the managers of the company to the need to exercise some control over coal production.[34] It was thought this was best achieved by the acquisition of coal lands. Unfortunately, by the end of 1875, the views of the management had changed in regard to unions. Although the cartel had been in operation for three years, the 1875 strike had proved "disastrous to the business of the Company." [35] In consequence, the successful stand of the railroad and the individual operators against the demands of the men was credited by the company with "permanently rescuing their property from the arbitrary control of an irresponsible trades union, which for so many years [had] interfered in and frequently dictated its management." [36] Control of production tributary to the lines was essential for any company that desired to be a major player in the cartel. In the case of the Reading, a regular revenue stream at cartel-supported prices was also essential to maintain its financial stability. Otherwise, the burden of interest payments, resulting from borrowing to fund its profligate coal-land purchases, would drag it down into insolvency, a state into which it finally sank in May 1880.[37]

In later years, and especially after the passage of the Interstate Commerce Commission Act in 1887, the cartel assumed a more informal aspect,[38] but there was little discernible difference in its actual operation.[39] After 1898, the "community of interest" developed under the guiding hand of J.P. Morgan and G.F. Baer employed the Temple Iron Company to absorb independently operated coal lands and prevent the construction of the New York, Wyoming and Western Railroad. This tightened still further the control of the major anthracite railroads over the industry as a whole.[40] In such an arrangement, there was no room for additional players, such as the UMWA, whose interests were not aligned with those of the operators.

There can be no doubt, therefore, that questions of power and control were at the heart of the conflict leading up to the 1902 strike, as Blatz[41] has already observed. There was more to it, however, than autocratic wealth and privilege versus the downtrodden and oppressed laboring poor, as the now expunged verse of the old hymn put it:

> The rich man in his castle
> The poor man at his gate
> God made them high and lowly
> And ordered their estate.

"Divine Right" Baer himself partly fell into this trap in his infamous statement about "the Christian men to whom God in his infinite wisdom has given the control of the property interests of the country." [42] Fortunately, the necessary assistance to the Almighty in His divine purposes was readily available in the form of the "successful management" of these property interests, on "which so much depends." [43] The perceived arrogance and presumption of such statements brought a justified outcry in the press and a clear signal that such unwarranted assertion of effectively feudal rights would not be tolerated by the public at large. Indeed, Baer would have served his cause better if he had abided by his own maxim "never to write where it was possible to avoid it." [44] Perhaps a better guide to the real motivation behind many of his actions and utterances can be found in his correspondence to Charles Steele:

> Beyond discharging my duty, I care very little for reputation: but I would be personally humiliated beyond conception if my management of these great properties should be similar to their past history. [45]

The need for management control of complex mining and transportation companies answerable to shareholders had grown steadily in the decades preceding the 1902 coal strike, until it reached a fully fledged corporate managerialism around the turn of the century. The initial diversity in corporate charters, [46] where some companies were common carriers and others had both railroad and mining privileges, had been replaced by a *de facto* standardized model of railroads with mining subsidiaries. The quest for control was a quest for stability in a fluctuating economic environment. If ruinous competition threatened this stability it would have to be eliminated, or at least regulated, by means of the cartel. If unions threatened regular shipments they would likewise have to be eliminated or neutralized as a disturbing force to management control. At the same time, a long line of operators from Ario Pardee onwards were happy to claim they had no objection to miners organizing themselves, provided this did not interfere in the management relationship between the operator and his employees. [47] Likewise, Baer, while denouncing the UMWA on the one side, was equally happy to assert:

> We must have the courage and the Christian heroism to denounce all oppression of labor, whether by capital or by labor itself. [48]

Hence a more private sense of justice and the rights of men in the personal philosophies of the operators sat a little uncomfortably alongside the public face of the hardened corporate manager, who carried the heavy responsibility of running a large-scale enterprise and delivering value to shareholders.

The Rule of Law

There can be no doubt that the operators viewed the rule of law as a key weapon in their arsenal to protect their property and personnel against damage and violence during periods of labor strife. Despite their substantial financial resources, which enabled them to deploy the best available legal counsel, they also had to contend with public opinion, and by extension the views of court juries, who were often felt to sympathize more with the cause of labor than their own. These issues will be explored in relation to two specific aspects of law enforcement during the period of the 1902 strike. The first of these is the use of the Coal and Iron Police; the second is the protection of employees from violence and intimidation.

The Coal and Iron Police have attracted much criticism and have readily been seen as the operators' chief vehicle for worker oppression. In part this may be the result of John Mitchell's well-known personal antagonism towards them and their deployment, as the "private standing army of the operators."[49] Likewise, other commentators, describing the period following the Mollie Maguire trials, state that "the Coal and Iron Police were kept intact and for a generation afterward remained the chief law enforcement agency in the region." [50] It would be all too easy for a reader to conclude from such statements that for several decades prior to the 1902 strike the coal regions were under the iron rule of near martial law, administered by hired uniformed thugs, answerable to no-one but the operators. However, such conclusions, even if expressed in milder terms, cannot be supported by the available evidence.

By an act of 27 February 1868, railroads were authorized to apply to the Governor to commission their own policemen. The individuals appointed had to take an oath and the commissions had to be recorded in every county through which the railroad passed. The commission conferred the same powers as those of Philadelphia policemen. A later act extended the above provisions to owners or lessors of collieries, whose policemen had to wear badges engraved with the words "Coal and Iron Policemen." Further to this, by 1902 at least, the prevailing legal opinion was that Coal and Iron Policemen should not go off the property they were employed to protect, for the purpose of assisting in arrests, without having a warrant.[51] After the 1900 strike, Attorney Wolverton had also made very clear to E.A. Oberrender of Coxe Brothers and Company, in the Lehigh Region, that a high standard of behavior was expected from these policemen:

> They should not do or show any violence any more than is necessary, and should never use their weapons of defense until absolutely necessary for their defense.[52]

Hence the Coal and Iron Police operated within quite a strict legal framework and had clear boundaries to their duties and responsibilities. Of course, if the worst elements of society from the slums of the larger cities were drafted into uniform and left to their own devices, there was no guarantee that high standards of discipline would be maintained, especially if confronted by a hostile mob. Such claims about the dubious backgrounds of policemen commissioned during the 1902 strike were made both by John Mitchell and by coal-region newspapers. However, Cornell's careful analysis of the 4000 commissions made during the strike indicate that only about 12% of them were to individuals from Philadelphia, the rest being from the coal regions or nearby communities.[53] Evidence from the Coxe Brothers' records tends to support Cornell's assessment. During the 1900 strike, for example, among the 47 policemen commissioned by the latter company were most of the senior officers of the company, including the superintendent, L.C. Smith, and E.A. Oberrender.[54] The latter was led to protest to Alexander B. Coxe directly in May of 1902 when he was directed to serve again as a policeman by Superintendent Smith. He argued:

> I believe that placing me in this position would be aggravating and antagonistic to the Hungarian uncivilised labor element, as I have been so conspicuous in these matters in the last strikes.[55]

Oberrender felt that his normal duties of looking after the estate land titles were much more important. He had taken up the matter directly with Mr Coxe, as he felt that if he tried to explain it to Mr Smith, the latter would "cut off the explanation by his usual insults." [56]

Quite apart from the tensions of Drifton office politics, guard duty was obviously not to the taste of all those who were called to serve!

The notion of a "standing army" also needs to be re-visited. While the actions of Coxe Brothers may not have been precisely replicated elsewhere, it is clear that the commissions of policemen were not continued any longer than necessary. As early as August 1902, Coxe Brothers revoked a number of commissions, followed by a large number more in the period September-December 1902.[57] Commissions were also revoked in cases of misconduct. One example of this was the somewhat unfortunate case of George Stock, who lost his position after being taken to court on questionable charges of indecent exposure and concealment of a deadly weapon. The charges were brought by John J. Hudock, who himself was being indicted on a conspiracy charge by the company for boycotting. According to Oberrender, "the court was evidently disgusted with the prosecution of this case"; Stock was acquitted of the weapons charge and received a mere $10 fine on the first charge, since he was a closely measured 347 feet from the nearest residence at the time![58] Much more seriously, four Coal and Iron Policemen were arrested after a boy was shot in the back at the Stanton Colliery, Wilkes-Barre, in June 1902.[59] It is therefore difficult to maintain that they were in any sense a law unto themselves, despite clearly being trigger-happy on several occasions.

John Mitchell further asserted of the Coal and Iron Police that "the services of these men are unnecessary and their presence unwarranted." [60] However the New York Times, which reported this statement, was unimpressed:

> This is a very foolish statement. The history of strikes, if it teaches anything at all, teaches the lesson that they are exceedingly apt to lead to violent and destructive acts on the part of the strikers.[61]

Following Mitchell's assertion, the president of the North American Coal Company, which operated the National Washery in Scranton, decided to take the UMWA president at his word. He wrote to Mitchell to say that he was starting his washery without any guards or policemen, as Mitchell had stated that they were unnecessary. Mitchell replied in writing that the company would not be molested in any way by members of the UMWA. Unfortunately, within a short time of starting up the washery it was dynamited and badly damaged. This left Mitchell open to two possible charges. The first was that he could not control the rank and file of his union. The second was that, if the perpetrators were not union members, then the union was not capable of maintaining discipline among the general populace and hence the policemen were indeed necessary.[62] This proved to be one of the few cases where an individual operator got the better of Mitchell.

The UMW Journal tried to characterize Coal and Iron Policemen as cold-blooded murderers and people who would place obstructions on railroad tracks to derail trains.[63] However, an individual, reported initially as having been shot dead by policemen in an incident at the William A Colliery in the Northern Field, may well have been shot from outside rather than inside the colliery stockade. This was revealed in subsequent press reports when the forensic evidence had been examined,[64] but this is not mentioned in the quote from the UMW Journal, nor is it mentioned by Cornell. The statement that policemen tried to derail trains appears to be without foundation and seems to be an attempt to shift the blame for incidents that <u>did</u> occur. For example, the Coxe Papers contain details of seven incidents when obstructions were placed on the tracks of the Delaware, Schuylkill and Susquehanna Railroad, including one case where the rock was so large it required three men to move it.[65]

The Coal Strike Commission's well-known conclusions about the Coal and Iron Policemen were that, while most were upright individuals, there were enough bad characters to discredit the entire body, and that overall their presence was an irritant and many of the disturbances during the strike grew out of their presence. Replacement by a constabulary appointed and paid by the county or state was recommended.[66] Arguably, however, these findings, which were quite favorable to the union's standpoint, overlooked two important issues. The first of these was that the Coal and Iron Police in general lacked training in dealing with violent or threatening situations and they were present in small numbers in dispersed and relatively isolated locations. This was in contrast to the imposing force of National Guard contingents such as the Philadelphia City Cavalry.[67] They were undoubtedly present at many disturbances, but in a number of cases it was prosecution of their lawful duties, rather than inflammatory behavior, that incurred the wrath of the mob. For example, when Coxe Brothers' policemen tried to arrest a violent stone-throwing striker, they themselves were assailed by a mob of 50-60 people, among whom, according to the court papers, it was the women who bombarded the policemen with stones.[68] The policemen would also be preferentially concentrated at flashpoints such as attempts to re-open mines or washeries. Casting the blame on the policemen for agitating the strikers may have been a convenient ploy by the union to divert attention from its own picketing activities. As the commission itself noted, places where good order was maintained "were mainly in the localities where the operators made no attempt to work the collieries." [69]

A second point concerns the establishment of a county or state constabulary. There is now strong evidence that the properly appointed local officers with a responsibility to preserve the peace were very tardy and reluctant in the prosecution of their duties during the strike, and in some cases tried to evade them altogether. For example, John Boyle, Burgess of Freeland, claimed that the local council had removed his authority over the police some time previously. Attorney Lenahan, retained by Coxe Bros., retorted that Boyle's statement "was all bosh" and that the duty of the burgess to maintain the peace could not be taken from him.[70] Lenahan also railed against the dilatoriness of these local officials more generally:

> I am kept busy night and day looking after the interests of non-union men whose rights have been outraged not only by the strikers, but by those very executive officers in the different boroughs whose duty it is to enforce the law but who are so strongly in sympathy with the strikers that they forget what they owe to their oaths and to their country.[71]

In such circumstances, the ruling of the commission seems somewhat unrealistic and it is unsurprising that the operators were keen to retain the services of their own legally appointed private policemen.

The very public denouncement of violence by the senior figures in the UMWA [72] was advantageous in maintaining a good media image for the union. It also seems they preferred to blame the Coal Iron Police when violence did break out rather than charge responsibility to elements in the populace who were not members of the UMWA. However, there was one type of intimidation from which they could not easily distance themselves, since their own officers were alleged to be directly involved. The type of intimidation in question was boycotting, which was used as a weapon against men who continued at work.

One particularly well-documented case was the so-called "Oneida boycott" which centered around workers at the Oneida breaker of Coxe Bros. and Company, who lived in the village of Sheppton, Schuylkill County. The method of implementing the boycott involved serving notice on shopkeepers, innkeepers, etc., not to provide goods or services to men who continued at work during the strike. Or if they did provide such services, to charge the men prices so exorbitant that it would take away all their wages.[73] A number of original boycott notices have survived to indicate that these were not merely verbal threats. One, for example, was served on a certain Jonathan Yost, innkeeper, directing him not to send food to men working at the breaker. Failure to abide by the order would result in complete loss of his trade, as union men would then take their custom elsewhere.[74] Apparently, such notices were served by a committee comprising, among others, one William Dettrey. Other participants in the boycott seem to have operated behind the guise of a sub-committee charged with distributing aid to strikers in need. John Hudock, signatory of the boycott notices, was a member of this sub-committee.[75] William Dettrey was the president of District Local 1513 of the UMWA and a member of the Executive Board of District Officers under Thomas Duffy.[76] Subsequently he was to be elected overall president of District 7.[77] During the strike he was active in visiting strike-breakers to try and persuade them to quit work and was arrested in August 1902 on charges of assault and battery, but subsequently acquitted. A hotelier also stated that Dettrey had placed a boycott on him for serving beer to working men.[78]

Boycotting of this kind was illegal and open to charges of conspiracy. On July 11, 1902, prosecutions were initiated on this basis against John Hudock and his sub-committee by Coxe Brothers. Although it is interesting to note that Dettrey, who had not signed the boycott notices himself, was not named in the list of those indicted. Hon. Charles N. Brumm, labor leader and ex-Congressman, together with Attorney Charles Snyder of Schuylkill County, tried to defuse the situation by offering to call the indicted men to their offices, inform them their (boycott) actions were illegal and advise them to abandon such practices.[79] However, Coxe Brothers persisted with the prosecution, only to find that out of a grand jury of 24 in Luzerne County, they could only count on "5 safe men," when they needed 12, and the position was similar in Schuylkill County. A safer route was to have the accused bound over for surety by a Schuylkill County judge. The practice in that county was to require outside security, unlike Luzerne County, where the defendants were generally bound over on their own recognizance.[80]

Although the financial and legal power of the operators may have been curtailed quite effectively by public opinion via the grand jury mechanism, the impact of the boycott on employees who chose to continue working was substantial. Thomas McNamara testified that he had to go seven miles to Hazleton for meat, as the Sheppton butcher would no longer sell to him, because he had been "visited by the UMWA committee."[81] A Coxe Brothers memo summed up the situation quite clearly:

> In Sheppton, a village of probably 400 inhabitants, by reason of its isolated location, it became so oppressive to the few loyal workmen of Oneida Colliery that it became necessary to provide transportation to such employees to go to distant parts for the necessaries of life.[82]

Coxe Brothers were also vigorous in their attempts to seek redress when employees were subject to other lines of violence and intimidation. For example, Albin Wassmer, Coxe Brothers' mining engineer, was seriously assaulted by a large mob of about 300 people in Freeland on July 1, 1902.[83] Superintendent Smith was extremely desirous of bringing the guilty parties to justice, writing as early as July 8:

> It is unfair to Mr Wassmer that his assault is not avenged. It shows a dilatory state of affairs upon our part and I want to push the matter faster.[84]

In response to these and other legal actions taken by the company, a suitably vitriolic reaction was forthcoming from the Hazleton-based "Trades Unionist":

> Since Smith took charge of the Railroad System he has exhibited a disposition that would compare better with that of a lunatic than a sane man as it relates to his treatment of the workmen, and it is under his orders now that the poor people who have been crushed for years by Coxe Brothers and Co. are being pursued and hounded with cold-blooded vindictiveness.[85]

(The railroad system referred to is the Delaware, Schuylkill and Susquehanna Railroad.)

This cycle of action, reaction and mutual recrimination engendered a very confrontational attitude between the operators and the local populace in parts of the Lehigh region. This was not helped by a limited number of evictions of striking workers from company houses and union charges of blacklisting by the operators.[86] However, it should not be assumed that the situation in the Lehigh region was exactly replicated elsewhere. In the Northern Field, for example, the Lackawanna Railroad claimed that 80% of its employees were actually opposed to the strike. Hence they were not at odds with the company, but had been forced to strike by a majority vote of the UMWA in other fields.[87] In the Schuylkill Region, R.C. Luther, general superintendent of the Philadelphia and Reading Coal and Iron Company, was most solicitous of the interests of the local population in areas tributary to the Reading Railroad. In a number of letters, he pressed the case for restoration of train services cut as a result of the strike, to avoid adverse public feeling, and the management of the railroad paid careful attention to his views.[88]

However, in the later part of the strike, company officers became increasingly nervous, as the scale of attacks on the Reading Railroad grew in number and severity. For example the tracks on the Silver Creek Branch were dynamited on multiple occasions. There was also more than one attempt to wreck the Lorberry miners' train between Lincoln and Pine Grove by wedging ties into trackside culverts. This was aimed at catching the down train on the heaviest grade, where it was most difficult to stop. Such was the potential for loss of life under these circumstances that Superintendent Garrett asserted that he would like to see the person responsible shot.[89]

Overall, the scale of violence against both persons and property makes it difficult to see how the operators could have responded with anything less in the way of security measures than was actually the case. Table 1, taken from a newspaper report at the beginning of October 1902, gives a partial list of "outrages" during the strike.[90] Apart from the number of fatalities and serious injuries, the extent of dynamiting of property and successful or attempted wrecking of trains is notable, because of the additional danger it presented to workmen and their families. The final tally of dynamitings was also significantly larger than that given in the table, since these and other types of incidents continued until the end of the strike.[91]

Commenting on the dynamiting of houses, Culin, that perspicacious observer from the National Guard, poignantly noted:

> This was intended merely as an admonition, it was said, with no personal harm, as dynamite explodes downward, without violence above. Alas! the wretched woman who brought her babe, sadly burned, to the General's headquarters, told a different story.[92]

The Right to Work

The operators' approach to protecting non-striking men was intimately bound up with a view about the right to work that found its most forceful proponent in G.F. Baer, but which was strongly opposed by John Mitchell. Beginning with the notion of equality of opportunity, Baer argued that:

> The great law that every laborer shall be protected in his inalienable right to labor must in all time be a well-proportioned pillar of free government.[93]

This statement was made prior to the strike, but a similar point was made by the well-known industrialist Abram Hewitt while the strike was in progress. Hewitt argued against the closed shop as a "denial of the right of every man to sell his labor in a free market" and the latter right, being inherent in man, could not be subject to arbitration.[94] Mitchell denied that the UMWA had ever sought to enforce a closed shop,[95] but he side-stepped the issue of whether intimidation, though not officially sanctioned by the union, could easily produce the same effect. Baer had made this point, arguing that through intimidation the workingman was "in terror of the ostracism, if not the personal violence, which follows an attempt to be a free man."[96] Likewise, the *Scranton Tribune* warned the union against any attempt "to interfere with personal liberty."[97] By contrast, Mitchell, with some support from clergy in the coal regions, argued that the right to work was not just an individual matter, because if it took the form of strike-breaking, which went against the wishes of the majority of the community, it was wrong.[98] Baer, in his final argument before the commission, characterised this issue as "Mr Mitchell's and Mr Gompers' new limitation of human freedom," i.e.

> A man who works during a strike has no moral right to work if his work destroys the hope and aspirations of his fellow men.[99]

Baer sharply observed that Mitchell and Gompers had avoided claiming that men had no legal right to work, invoking instead some higher, undefined moral right. He disputed their ability to determine whether the work of an individual would destroy the hopes and aspirations of his fellows.[100] His argument carried the day with the commission, if not with all sections of public opinion. It ruled that:

> Approval of the object of a strike ... cannot sanction an attempt to destroy the right of others to a different opinion in this respect.[101]

Likewise the commission fully appreciated that issues surrounding the right to work, and its enforcement or prevention lay at the very heart of the contest between the two parties:

> There can be no doubt that without threats, intimidation, and violence toward those who would otherwise be willing to remain at work, or take the places of those who had ceased to work, the coercion of employers, which a strike always contemplates, would be less potent in compelling acquiescence in its demands. This is the danger point of the whole matter.[102]

The Approach to the Strike

In addition to their broad agreement on underlying principles, the operators also adopted a number of common tactical positions during the strike to bolster their case in the face of much adverse public opinion. These can be characterized as follows:

- The need for solidarity under threat
- Problems of productivity and discipline since the 1900 strike
- The contention that the UMWA was a bituminous organization controlled in the interest of bituminous operators
- The reluctance to submit to arbitration

These tactical positions will now be examined in turn. Space unfortunately precludes consideration of operators' views on other specific issues such as dockage and the size of mine cars, but informative discussion of these topics can be found in earlier studies.[103]

Solidarity under threat

In considering the approach to the strike by the operators, it is important to remember that their public face, often regarded as intransigent and arrogant, reflected the negotiating stance of a group of able and experienced corporate managers against the most articulate and skilful representative of labor to emerge in a generation. During the spring of 1902, they were also not looking for quick compromise, as it appears they did not believe that a strike would actually take place.[104] This made it harder to backtrack subsequently when the strike had begun, as concessions would immediately be regarded as a sign of weakness.

The first step therefore was to build up solidarity. As Baer remarked to fellow presidents Thomas and Truesdale just after the collapse of April negotiations with the UMWA and the National Civic Federation, "I believe that if we stand solid and firm, we will win." [105] The process of developing a common approach to the UMWA had begun earlier, and certainly by the time of the sequence of letters sent by the presidents to Mitchell in February 1902. These letters were in response to Mitchell's invitation for them to attend a joint conference in Scranton on March 12. [106] In some cases, if not all, the presidents had clearly circulated draft copies of these letters to each other before sending them to Mitchell. [107] Nevertheless, in his May letter quoted above, Baer had stressed that these letters expressed the individual judgement of each president. Therefore the letters presented a stronger case than could be achieved by producing a single document signed by all the presidents. The letters were duly published in June in the press. [108]

From these letters the initial outline of several major arguments began to emerge. These arguments would be developed during the course of the strike. The first of these was the familiar point about the desire to deal with their own employees rather than an outside organization. The second was the impracticability of uniform wage scales across the entire anthracite region, because of the wide variation in mining conditions. However, two further issues also began to come to the fore. One of these was the problem of discipline in the mines, the other was the concern about the UMWA being an organization controlled by the interests of the bituminous industry.

Problems of prouctivity and discipline

The case for discipline in the mines was a strong one from the outset. It was used in a telling manner to counter claims made by the UMWA about the effectiveness of industrial relations after coalfields were unionized. None made the case more forcefully than President Thomas of the Erie. He stated that after the UMWA became established in the anthracite regions, between April and October 1, 1901, there were 102 interruptions of work occasioned by "unwarranted demands," resulting in the loss of 900 days of work and over 600,000 tons of production. [109] President Baer weighed in on the same theme, arguing that "you cannot have discipline when the employee disregards and disobeys the reasonable orders and directions in the conduct of business of his superior officer, relying upon some outside power to sustain him." [110]

Both presidents also linked their arguments about discipline to a wider question about reductions in productivity. Baer claimed that the efficacy of the Coal and Iron Company's mines had declined by 1 million tons, or 12.5% per miner, while Thomas stated that a 12% reduction in output per man had taken place. [111] This reduction in productivity more than offset the 10% pay rise awarded after the 1900 strike, they argued. This made UMWA claims about low wages difficult to justify, since the men appeared to have responded to a pay rise by working proportionately less![112]

The UMWA—a bituminous organisation?

The issue of the control of the UMWA by bituminous interests, began as a counter to the UMWA claim for uniform pay rates across the anthracite regions. The operators argued that mining conditions varied so greatly within and between mines and coal basins in anthracite that this was not possible. The commission eventually concurred with the operators on this point.[113] However, the latter subsequently developed the bituminous mining question into a quite effective counter to the argument that the UMWA was an appropriate body to negotiate on behalf of the anthracite miners. In its submission to the commission, the Pennsylvania Coal Company argued that the overwhelming majority of members of the UMWA were engaged in the mining of bituminous coal, which was in "active, keen and increasing competition with anthracite." [114] Hence, every advance in the cost of production of anthracite benefitted the bituminous industry. Similarly, Baer, in his earlier statement to senators Quay and Penrose on September 3, 1902, had argued that wages could not be increased without pushing up prices and higher prices would drive the public to use bituminous coal.[115] He returned to this theme in his closing argument before the commission, stressing that the UMWA had to keep the bituminous men at work, so they could be taxed to provide the strike fund for the anthracite men![116] Interestingly, this presented a problem for the UMWA themselves, as one of their internal circulars revealed. In June 1902 the headquarters of District 2 in Clearfield, Pennsylvania, found that large shipments of bituminous coal were retarding the chances of the anthracite miners terminating their struggle, so an output restriction placing them on a four-day week had to be established.[117] This was clearly a delicate balancing act, since reduced time also implied reduced contributions to the strike fund for the anthracite men. While the UMWA may have aimed to avoid prolonging the strike, the anthracite operators claimed that their bituminous counterparts (operators, not miners) made liberal contributions to the anthracite strike fund, to try and extend the advantages accruing to the bituminous industry for as long as possible.[118]

Arguments such as these, which had significant logical force, and which were not really countered by the UMWA, reflected the increasing sophistication of the operators' position as the strike wore on. It also helped in some measure to deflect the widespread public criticism of their policy of opposition to arbitration. Baer's statement to senators Quay and Penrose is a good example of this. Aspects of both the bituminous competition issue and the arbitration question were included in his statement, which received at least qualified approval from some sections of the press.

The reluctance to submit to arbitration

The operators' opposition to arbitration neatly summarizes many aspects of their approach to the strike. Cornell condenses Baer's presentation of their position into four points that were not deemed subject to arbitration:

1. A question of wages when an increase would destroy the business
2. The right of employers to select their own employees
3. The right of companies to protect their property and workers from mob rule of labor organizations
4. A question as to whether the business was to be managed by the owners or a labor organization [119]

He also charts the detailed history of the operators' slowly shifting position, that finally culminated in acceptance of the establishment of the Coal Strike Commission, albeit after immense pressure had been applied from the highest political and financial levels in the country. Hence this does not need to be repeated here.

Going beyond specific issues, it was perhaps Commissioner Carroll D. Wright who really saw to the heart of the matter in his brief analysis of the strike during June 1902. In his report to the president he concluded that

> there is no confidence existing between the employees and their employers and suspicion lurks in the mind of everyone and distrust in every action on either side.[120]

Divergent Views of the Economics of the Anthracite Business

As mentioned earlier, the letters of the operators, which had been written in February 1902, were published in June of that year. Partly in response to this, John Mitchell subsequently published an "address to the public," in which he attempted to refute a number of the arguments of the operators. In addition to specific reference to the evils of dockage and the miners' ton, he made claims about low wages and argued that productivity had risen, not fallen, since unionization. He further charged that, by means of exorbitant freight rates, the railroad departments of the companies absorbed profits that should have been attributed to the coal companies, making them appear to operate at a loss.[121] The wages question was to receive exhaustive treatment in the commission's final report, but little further was said about the question of productivity or exorbitant freight rates. Later writers have similarly referred to Mitchell's claims but none have subjected them to any further investigation. Constraints of length unfortunately preclude detailed examination of all three issues here. However, the third one, concerning freight rates, will be pursued because it went to the heart of the economics of the anthracite business and directly concerned the dual role of the major operators, as presidents of both railroads and mining companies. It is also of particular interest, because the commission refused to admit evidence pertaining to it as relevant to its deliberations, despite the protestations of Henry Demarest Lloyd.[122]

The origins of Mitchell's views on freight rates can be traced back at least as far as 1901, to his testimony before the Industrial Commission.[123] The way the matter is described is very reminiscent of the words of Roberts, whose treatise on the anthracite coal industry was published in the same year. So it may be that Roberts is the original source for Mitchell's thinking, although it was the latter who introduced into his 1901 testimony the idea that the freight rates were "excessive." By 1902, "excessive" had become "exorbitant" in his open letter to the public, although no evidence in support of his assertions was ever produced.[124] Baer was quick to pick up on this point. An offer was made to the UMWA during the strike to open his company's books for inspection, but the offer was not taken up.[125] This was a clever move by Baer, because he knew the weak financial performance of both the railroad and the Coal and Iron Company over many years would make it easy for him to demonstrate penury. He was not the first Reading president to use this tactic, as it had previously been deployed by Austin Corbin during the 1887–88 labor troubles. Corbin issued figures in January 1888 which stated that during the period January 1, 1876 – January 1, 1888, the company had paid the miners $57 million in wages, but had received less than $45 million for selling the coal the miners produced.[126] Table 2 shows a summary analysis of the profits and losses of the railroad and Coal and Iron Company in the period prior to the 1902 strike, and the net outturn of the two companies combined.[127] The figures are taken from the annual reports and have been totalled (not averaged) over a decade. Alternative ending years of 1900 and 1901 are shown, since 1901 was unusual for the Coal and Iron Company, though not for the railroad, in being the only year since its formation when profits exceeded $1 million.[128] These figures would seem to substantiate Roberts' statement that the railroads lost money on mining operations, but returns on freight recouped them.[129] Indeed, the railroad's own commentary on its financial performance for the year 1895 says the same thing.[130] However, Mitchell's charge of exorbitant freight rates is difficult to support, as Baer would well have known, because there is no sign of the excess profits that presumably would have resulted, if rates had indeed been exorbitant. The average profit of the joint operations was only about $30,000 or $75,000 a year depending on the choice of decade window. This can hardly be classified as an impressive return on the enormous investment represented by the railroad, not to mention the mines and coal lands of the Coal and Iron Company.

These annual figures also need to be compared with the cost of a 10% increase in mining wages. In 1901, mining coal and repairs cost the Coal and Iron Company $12.43 million, according to its published income account.[131] Since nearly 78% of the cost of coal in cars was attributable to labor in that year,[132] approximately $9.6 million must have been spent on wages. A 10%

increase on this bill would have been about $80,000 a <u>month</u>. This was more than the <u>annual</u> average profit of the joint operations. Since the coal strike produced a knock-on effect to railroad wages, the 10% advance for these employees approved in November 1902, added a further $99,000 to the monthly figure for the miners.[133] The previous financial history of the company gave no grounds for believing that increases of this magnitude could be met without raising coal prices and freight rates. Hence Baer was able to conclude in his letter to Truesdale and Thomas "there is not an officer in our employ who does not heartily concur in the soundness of the conclusions we have reached,"[134] namely that wage increases could not be afforded.

There were certainly long-standing issues about the fairness of relative freight rates on anthracite and bituminous coal,[135] and about treatment of independent operators by some railroads.[136] However, no evidence of inflating the freight rates charged to mining subsidiaries for the benefit of the parent railroads has come to light to support Mitchell's assertions. On the contrary, other testimony at the same Industrial Commission hearings in 1901, albeit by General Superintendent Luther of the Coal and Iron Company, stated that they paid "an established and agreed rate of freight, an established rate." In response to further questioning, Luther added "I think we pay the same as other shippers do exactly."[137]

Baer laid down the gauntlet of access to the books of the Reading Company, but Mitchell declined to pick up, doubtless because he had seen enough of Baer's figures to fear he might be correct. In so doing, Baer had made a very effective move on behalf of the operators. However, if Mitchell had been a closer student of railroad finance, he might have been able to press the point in relation not just to annual profits, but accumulated revenue surpluses. This is a large topic, which is examined in much more detail in a forthcoming study of the anthracite industry,[138] but some salient points can be mentioned here.

Accumulated revenue surpluses were sums left over after payments of all fixed charges and stockholders dividends. Well-managed and prudent companies might expect to build up such surpluses in good years as a financial buffer against adverse economic circumstances in the future. Poorly managed companies, or those that had overstretched themselves, might barely manage to pay dividends in good years, leaving no surplus to hedge against the bad. They would also have the specter of receivership hanging over them for extended periods. By the turn of the century the major players in the anthracite coal combination fell into two groups, in terms of financial strength, a point that has largely escaped previous commentators on the coal strike. Among the weaker brethren on the above criteria were the Reading, the Lehigh Valley and the Erie, while the stronger companies included the Lackawanna and the Delaware and Hudson.

By 1901, after 3 receiverships,[139] the Reading had finally recovered from its over-investment in partially unproductive coal lands in the 1870s to a sufficient degree that its revenue surplus had increased to $3.87 million. Half of that was due to the success of the business in 1901 alone, however, and the Annual Report was quite particular in noting that this surplus was not available for distribution to shareholders without weakening the company.[140] Since it was also a non-recurrent amount, any use of it to meet recurrent expenditure such as wage claims would cause it to evaporate rapidly, leaving the company in jeopardy. The position of the Lehigh Valley was significantly worse, as it had no revenue reserve in 1901 and posted a substantial loss on its combined railroad and coal operations.[141] It is therefore not surprising that in his statement to senators Quay and Penrose, Baer was quick to draw attention to the Reading, Lehigh Valley and Erie Railroads who "had not paid dividends on their stock for years." [142]

In contrast, the Delaware and Hudson, which had been reasonably transparent in reporting its financial situation over the preceding two decades, had managed to maintain a revenue surplus of between $5 million and $7 million in every year from 1888–1901, with the exception of 1898.[143]

The Lackawanna maintained a veil of secrecy over its financial position by failing to produce published annual reports over more than three decades of the presidency of Samuel Sloan, which ended in 1899. When the veil was finally lifted, it became clear that the Lackawanna, alone among the anthracite carriers, if the Pennsylvania Railroad is left aside, was truly in a financial league of its own. Its revenue surplus had climbed to $16.7 million by the end of 1901.[144] It is apparent therefore that not only could President Truesdale of the Lackawanna have sat out an almost indefinite strike, but he could readily afford any likely pay settlement for the miners, with or without any corresponding increase in the price of coal. It is hardly surprising, therefore, that he took a very retiring position in the strike negotiations, leaving his more impecunious and therefore more intransigent presidential colleagues to carry the brunt of the negotiations! Seemingly Mitchell did not attempt to divide the operators in terms of their financial standing and concentrate his fire on the Northern Field companies with ample or overflowing coffers. That said, had he attempted the tactic it might well have backfired, because of the claimed opposition of the vast majority of the Lackawanna's employees to the strike, as has already been noted. That opposition was doubtless partly due to the 30% increase in pay that the Lackawanna miners had received in 1901, as compared to 1900.[145]

Conclusion

It is perhaps a tribute to the judgement of the Anthracite Coal Strike Commission that both sides in the conflict were able to claim a substantial measure of victory. From the operators' perspective, the sliding scale was re-introduced, the demand for uniform rates of pay had not succeeded, recognition of the UMWA had not been mandated and the pay increases were no more than expected.[146] Both sides had the mettle and determination to fight the other to a standstill, which they duly did. Each side had an able and effective orator to put their case, the one the darling of the public and the press, the other pilloried for his sanctimonious utterances early in the strike, but partially re-habilitated in the later stages as a result of more effective and telling arguments. Yet the operators had one last card that they played almost unnoticed during the strike and seemingly without reaction from the union or indeed the commission. They took the opportunity to intensify their capital investment in new equipment in the breakers. This reduced the need to employ outside labor. At the breakers of Coxe Brothers alone, the jobs of 296 men and boys were replaced by mechanical equipment for sorting and sizing coal. Of this total, 82 jobs were lost at Drifton, 80 at Derringer and 66 at Oneida.[147] Similarly, the advent of the electrically operated breaker with mechanical slate-picking machinery, at the Auchincloss mine in Nanticoke, coincided precisely with the early days of the strike. This led the *Scranton Tribune* to forecast the eventual loss of 20,000 breaker boy jobs as the technology spread through the coal regions.[148] While a welcome development to those who railed against the "evil of child labor,"[149] it would also rid the operators of a troublesome and unreliable element in the union.[150]

Unlike new capital investment, which benefitted the operators, the abandonment of five mines in the Shenandoah area during the strike, owing to flooding, was a loss to both sides. Four of these mines belonged to the Coal and Iron Company and the capital loss totaled $1.5 million.[151]

A final tally of the financial effects of strikes over the first 31 years of unionization in the coal regions, 1900–1931, perhaps gives pause for thought. According to the calculations of the Hudson Coal Company, at least, wage benefits from strikes were more than outweighed by lost earnings from inactivity or reduced demand, when high wages made coal prices uncompetitive.[152] Set against this, however, were a wide range of improvements in working practices and conditions that began with the rulings of the Anthracite Coal Strike Commission.

Table 1
"Partial List of Outrages from the *New York Tribune*"

Killed	14	Riots	69
Severely injured	42	Works dynamited	6
Shot from ambush	16	Trains dynamited	1
Aggravated assault	67	Railroad bridges dynamited	4
Attempts to lynch	1	Railroads seized	5
Houses dynamited	12	Trains wrecked	6
Houses burned	3	Attempted wrecks	9
Buildings burned	10	Trains attacked	7
Washeries burned	3	Strikes in schools	14
Stockades burned	2		

Table 2
Total Net Profits and Losses (in thousands of dollars) by the Philadelphia and Reading Railroad and the Philadelphia and Reading Coal and Iron Company in the period prior to the 1902 strike

	Railroad	Coal and Iron	Total (both Co's)
Time Period	Net Out turn	Net Out turn	Net Out turn
1892 – 1901	2,593 Profit	1,836 Loss	757 Profit
1891 – 1900	4,620 Profit	4,316 Loss	303 Profit

N.B. A change in the financial year end during the period means that there is a very small element of double-counting in the figures.

Notes

1. P. Roberts, *The Anthracite Coal Industry* (New York: The Macmillan Company, 1901), 254.

2. B. Folsom, *The Myth of the Robber Barons: A New Look at the Rise of Big Business in America* (Herndon, VA: Young America's Foundation, 1987).

3. P.K. Blatz, *Democratic Miners: Work and Labor Relations in the Anthracite Coal Industry, 1875–1925* (Albany, NY: State University of New York Press, 1994).

4. R.J. Cornell, *The Anthracite Coal Strike of 1902* (Washington, DC: Catholic University of America Press, 1957).

5. C.K. Yearley, *Enterprise and Anthracite: Economics and Democracy in Schuylkill County, 1820–75* (Baltimore, MD: Johns Hopkins Press, 1961).

6. Hudson Coal Company, *The Story of Anthracite* (New York: Hudson Coal Company, 1932).

7. J.S. Harris, *Report of Joseph S. Harris on the Coal Lands of the Philadelphia and Reading Coal and Iron Company* (Philadelphia: Jackson Bros., 1880).

8. Pennsylvania Railroad, *Report of the Investigating Committee of the Pennsylvania Railroad Company* (Philadelphia, PA: Allen, Lane and Scott, 1974).

9. U.S. Anthracite Coal Strike Commission, *Report to the President on the Anthracite Coal Strike of May–October, 1902* (Washington, DC: Government Printing Office, 1903), 256. (Hereafter referred to as Report of the Anthracite Coal Strike Commission)

10. U.S. Industrial Commission, *Report of the Industrial Commission on the Relations and Conditions of Capital and Labor Employed in the Mining Industry*, Volume XII (Washington, DC: Government Printing Office, 1901), 701.

11. Roberts, *The Anthracite Coal Industry*, 203.

12. *Board of Directors Minutes*, Pennsylvania Coal Company, 17 Nov 1851, State Archives, Harrisburg.

13. E. Jones, *The Anthracite Coal Combination in the United States* (Cambridge, MA: Harvard University Press, 1914).

14. For a discussion of such transportation contracts, see, for example, W.R. Storrs to S. Sloan, 11 Nov, 25 Nov 1881, Letterbook 32A, Delaware, Lackawanna and Western Railroad Coal Department Papers, Lackawanna County Historical Society.

15. Calculated from data in F.E. Saward, *The Coal Trade for 1903* (New York, NY: F.E. Saward, 1903), 26.

16. Ibid., 21.

17. *Report of the Industrial Commission*, 700.

18. C.P. Foulke and W.G. Foulke, *Calvin Pardee 1841–1923: His Family and His Enterprises* (Philadelphia: The Pardee Company, 1979), 77.

19. R.T. Berthoff, "The Social Order of the Anthracite Region, 1825–1902," *Pennsylvania Magazine of History and Biography* 89, July 1965, 261–91, 281.

20. W. Mailly, "The Anthracite Coal Strike," *International Socialist Review* III, August 1 1902, 79–85.

21. W.N. Appel (compiler), *Addresses and Writings of George F. Baer* (Lancaster, PA: privately printed, 1916), 255.

22. G.F. Baer to J. Mitchell, 18 Feb 1902, Baer Letterbooks, Reading Company Papers, Hagley Library, Wilmington, DE.

23. Quoted in Foulke, *Calvin Pardee*, 76.

24. U.S. Congress, House of Representatives, *Labor Troubles in the Anthracite Regions of Pennsylvania 1887–88*, Report 4147, 50th Congress, 2nd Session (Washington, DC: Government Printing Office, 1889), 554–55.

25. W.T. Lewis to E.B. Coxe, 23 Nov 1887, Box 553, Coxe Family Mining Papers, Historical Society of Pennsylvania.

26. G.F. Baer to J. Mitchell, 9 May 1902, Baer Letterbooks, Reading Company Papers.

27. Cornell, *The Anthracite Coal Strike of 1902*, 90.

28. Blatz, *Democratic Miners*, 131–32.

29. G.F. Baer to E.B. Thomas and W.H. Truesdale, 2 May 1902, Baer Letterbooks, Reading Company Papers.

30. M.W. Schlegel, *Ruler of the Reading: The Life of Franklin B. Gowen 1836–1889* (Harrisburg, PA: Archives Publishing Company, 1947).

31. Jones, *Anthracite Coal Combination*.

32. *Annual Report of the Philadelphia and Reading Railroad* (P&RRR) for 1895, 19.

33. *Annual Report of the P&RRR for 1871*, 16–17.

34. Ibid.

35. *Annual Report of the P&RRR for 1875*, 16.

36. Ibid., 17.

37. *Annual Report of the P&RRR for 1882*, 24.

38. Jones, *Anthracite Coal Combination*, 49.

39. G. Virtue, "The Anthracite Combinations," *Quarterly Journal of Economics* 10, April 1896, 296–323, 322.

40. Jones, *Anthracite Coal Combination*, 67, 77, 215–16.

41. Blatz, *Democratic Miners*, 120.

42. Cornell, *The Anthracite Coal Strike of 1902*, 170, quoting original Baer Letter in Mitchell Papers.

43. Ibid.
44. G.F. Baer to E.B. Thomas and W.H. Truesdale, 2 May 1902, Baer Letterbooks, Reading Company Papers.
45. G.F. Baer to Charles Steele, 3 Jan 1902, Box B-642, Reading Company Papers.
46. S.P. Adams, "Different Charters, Different Paths: Corporations and Coal in Antebellum Pennsylvania and Virginia," *Business and Economic History* 27, 1998, 1, 78–90.
47. *Labor Troubles in the Anthracite Regions of Pennsylvania 1887–88*, 555.
48. Appel, *Addresses and Writings of George F. Baer*, 257.
49. John Mitchell, reported in the *Scranton Tribune*, 4 June 1902. (All articles referenced in this paper from the *Scranton Tribune* can be found in the Enderlin Collection, Hagley Library.)
50. D.L. Miller and R.E. Sharpless, *The Kingdom of Coal: Work, Enterprise and Ethnic Communities in the Mine Fields* (Philadelphia: University of Pennsylvania Press, 1985), 158–59.
51. S.P. Wolverton to E.A. Oberrender, 10 May 1902, Coxe Family Mining Papers, Box 560.
52. S.P. Wolverton to E.A. Oberrender, 23 Jan 1901, Coxe Family Mining Papers, Box 555.
53. Cornell, *The Anthracite Coal Strike of 1902*, 161.
54. E.A. Oberrender to R.G. McMichael, 27 Nov 1900; E.A. Oberrender to L.C. Smith, 27 Oct 1900, Coxe Family Mining Papers, Box 555.
55. E.A. Oberrender to Alex. B. Coxe, 25 May 1902, Coxe Family Mining Papers, Box 561.
56. Ibid.
57. Folders 14 and 20, Box 555, Coxe Family Mining Papers.
58. E.A. Oberrender to L.C. Smith, 11 Sept 1902.
59. *Scranton Tribune*, 6 June 1902.
60. *New York Times*, 8 June 1902.
61. Ibid.
62. *Scranton Tribune*, 1 Sept, 4 Sept 1902.
63. Quoted in Cornell, *The Anthracite Coal Strike of 1902*, 161.
64. *Scranton Tribune*, 3 July 1902.
65. Box 560, Coxe Family Mining Papers.
66. *Report of the Anthracite Coal Strike Commission*, 84.
67. S. Culin, *A Trooper's Narrative of Service in the Anthracite Coal Strike, 1902* (Philadelphia: George W. Jacobs and Co., 1903), 68. Box 560, Coxe Family Mining Papers.
69. *Report of the Anthracite Coal Strike Commission*, 74.
70. E.A. Oberrender to L.C. Smith, 1 Oct, 7 Oct 1902, Box 560, Coxe Family Mining Papers.
71. J.T. Lenahan to L.C. Smith, 6 Oct 1902, Box 560, Coxe Family Mining Papers.
72. *Report of the Anthracite Coal Strike Commission*, 74.
73. E.A. Oberrender to L.C. Smith, 16 June 1902, Box 560, Coxe Family Mining Papers.
74. Boycott notices, Box 562, Coxe Family Mining Papers.
75. E.A. Oberrender to L.C. Smith, 19 July 1902, Box 561, Coxe Family Mining Papers.
76. *Trades Unionist*, 25 July 1902.
77. Blatz, *Democratic Miners*, 173.
78. E.A. Oberrender to L.C. Smith, 30 June 1902, Box 560; E.A. Oberrender to L.C. Smith, 20 Oct 1902, Box 561; W.A. Evans to L.C. Smith, 30 Sept 1902, Box 560, Coxe Family Mining Papers.

79. E.A. Oberrender to L.C. Smith, 18 July 1902, Box 560, Coxe Family Mining Papers.

80. E.A. Oberrender to L.C. Smith, 27 Aug, 29 Aug 1902, Box 560, Coxe Family Mining Papers.

81. Transcript of Testimony of Thos. McNamara, 16 July 1902, Commonwealth vs. Stephen Drosdick and Edward Malloy, Box 560, Coxe Family Mining Papers.

82. Boycott Folder, Box 561, Coxe Family Mining Papers.

83. Statement of A. Wassmer to E.A. Oberrender, 1 July 1902, Box 561, Coxe Family Mining Papers.

84. L.C. Smith to E.A. Oberrender, 8 July 1902, Box 561, Coxe Family Mining Papers.

85. *Trades Unionist*, 25 July 1902.

86. L. C. Smith to E. A. Oberrender, 4 July 1902, Box 560, Coxe Family Mining Papers; Trades Unionist, 25 July 1902.

87. *Report of the Anthracite Coal Strike Commission*, 103.

88. Correspondence, B-454, Reading Company Papers.

89. W.A. Garrett to T.Vorhees, 6 Oct, 7 Oct 1902, B-454, Reading Company Papers.

90. Source for Table 1: Clipping from *The Sun*, 4 Oct 1902, Box 560, Coxe Family Mining Papers.

91. W.A. Garrett to T. Vorhees, 24 Oct 1902, B-454, Reading Company Papers.

92. Culin, A *Trooper's Narrative*, 40.

93. Appel, *Addresses and Writings of George F. Baer*, 257.

94. Cornell, *The Anthracite Coal Strike of 1902*, 127.

95. Ibid., 128.

96. Appel, *Addresses and Writings of George F. Baer*, 257.

97. *Scranton Tribune*, 5 June 1902.

98. D. Doukas, "Corporate Capitalism on Trial: The Hearings of The Anthracite Coal Strike Commission, 1902–1903," *Identities–Newark* 3, 1997, 3, 367–398, 380.

99. Appel, *Addresses and Writings of George F. Baer*, 329.

100. Ibid., 330.

101. *Report of the Anthracite Coal Strike Commission*, 76.

102. Ibid., 74.

103. Cornell, *The Anthracite Coal Strike of 1902*; Blatz, *Democratic Miners*; Doukas, "Corporate Capitalism on Trial."

104. Appel, *Addresses and Writings of George F. Baer*, 343; Cornell, *The Anthracite Coal Strike of 1902*, 87.

105. G.F. Baer to E.B. Thomas and W.H. Truesdale, 2 May 1902, Baer Letterbooks, Box 642, Reading Company Papers.

106. Cornell, *The Anthracite Coal Strike of 1902*, 75.

107. G.F. Baer to W.H. Truesdale, 19 Feb 1902, Baer Letterbooks Box 642, Reading Company Papers.

108. *New York American and Journal*, 11 June 1902, copy in Box 560, Coxe Family Mining Papers.

109. *Report of the Anthracite Coal Strike Commission*, 220.

110. Ibid., 218.

111. Ibid., 218, 220.

112. Ibid., 115.

113. Ibid., 71.

114. Ibid., 113.

115. Cornell, *The Anthracite Coal Strike of 1902*, 132; unattributed clipping with text of Baer statement, Box 560, Coxe Family Mining Papers.

116. Appel, *Addresses and Writings of George F. Baer*, 338–39.

117. P. Gilday and R. Gilbert, UMWA District 2 Circular, copy in B-454, Reading Com-

pany Papers.

118. *Report of the Anthracite Coal Strike Commission*, 62.

119. Cornell, *The Anthracite Coal Strike of 1902*, 133

120. C.D. Wright, Report to the President on Anthracite Coal Strike, *Bulletin of the Department of Labor, No. 43* (Washington, DC: Government Printing Office, 1902), 1165.

121. *Scranton Tribune*, 23 June 1902; Cornell, *The Anthracite Coal Strike of 1902*, 111.

122. Doukas, "Corporate Capitalism on Trial," 383.

123. *Report of the Industrial Commission*, 200–01.

124. *Scranton Tribune*, 23 June 1902.

125. Appel, *Addresses and Writings of George F. Baer*, 323.

126. *Philadelphia Times*, 23 Jan 1888, clipping in Box 553, Coxe Family Mining Papers.

127. Source for Table 2: *Annual Reports of the Philadelphia and Reading Railroad and the Reading Company* for 1891–1901.

128. *Annual Reports of the Philadelphia and Reading Railroad and Reading Company* for 1891–1901.

129. Roberts, *The Anthracite Coal Industry*, 76.

130. *Annual Report of the Philadelphia and Reading Railroad* for 1895, 11.

131. *Annual Report of the Reading Company* for 1901, 45.

132. Calculated from data in Wright, Report to the President on Anthracite Coal Strike, 1158.

133. *Board of Directors Minutes*, Philadelphia and Reading Railway, 19 Nov 1902.

134. G.F. Baer to W.H. Truesdale and E.B. Thomas, 2 May 1902, Baer Letterbooks, Box 642, Reading Company Papers.

135. F.B. Gowen, Argument of Mr. Franklin B. Gowen, For Complainants, Interstate Commerce Commission No. 150, Coxe Brothers and Co. vs. The Lehigh Valley Railroad Co., March 19 and 20, 1889 (Philadelphia: Allen, Lane and Scott, 1889), 16–17.

136. E.B. Coxe to G.B. Roberts, 14 Nov 1887, Box 458, Coxe Family Mining Papers.

137. *Report of the Industrial Commission*, 650.

138. R.G. Healey (forthcoming), *From the Civil War to the 1902 Coal Strike: Recession and Resurgence in the Pennsylvanian Anthracite Coal Industry* (Scranton PA: University of Scranton Press).

139. S. Daggett, *Railroad Reorganization* (New York: A.M. Kelley, 1908, reprint).

140. *Annual Report of the Reading Company* for 1901, 8; for 1900, 5.

141. *Annual Reports of the Lehigh Valley Railroad* for 1901, 1902.

142. Unattributed newspaper clipping, Box 560, Coxe Family Mining Papers.

143. *Annual Reports of the Delaware and Hudson Canal Company* for 1888–1898; *Annual Reports of the Delaware and Hudson Company* for 1899–1901.

144. *Annual Report of the Delaware, Lackawanna and Western Railroad* for 1901, 14.

145. Ibid., 10.

146. Blatz, *Democratic Miners*, 171; *Report of the Anthracite Coal Strike Commission*, 80–83.

147. Undated clipping from *Hazelton Daily Standard*, Box 560, Coxe Family Mining Papers.

148. *Scranton Tribune*, 30 April 1902.

149. P. Roberts, *Anthracite Coal Communities* (New York: Macmillan, 1904), 175.

150. *Report of the Anthracite Coal Strike Commission*, 62.

151. *Scranton Tribune*, 7 August 1902.

152. Hudson Coal Company, *The Story of Anthracite* (New York: Hudson Coal Company, 1932), 308.

John Mitchell
and the Anthracite Coal Strike of 1902:
A Century Later

Joseph M. Gowaskie

One hundred years ago some 150,000 anthracite mine workers engaged in a titanic struggle with some of the most powerful corporations in the United States. As we know from Robert J. Cornell's outstanding work, the mine workers, led by 32-year-old John Mitchell, remained on strike for over five and a half months until public and political pressure forced President Theodore Roosevelt to intervene and appoint a commission accepted by both parties to investigate the industry and issue an award resolving the dispute.[1]

In addition to Cornell's fine study, other scholars have carefully investigated the anthracite industry, the state of labor relations between the mine workers and the operators, and the attempts by the United Mine Workers of America (UMWA) to organize the mine workers into its ranks.[2] Mitchell's efforts in this process has been chronicled by several historians, including yours truly who spent over a year of his life pouring over the 220-odd boxes of Mitchell Papers in the Catholic University of America archives.[3] While the scholarly output on Mitchell is extensive and solid, he still remains something of an enigma, as there are several features of his life that are contradictory and puzzling, making it difficult, if not impossible, to arrive at a balanced and objective evaluation of his life and work. This paper will re-examine some of the salient aspects of Mitchell's career, especially emphasizing his relationship with the anthracite mine workers, and placing that relationship within the context of his entire career. Hopefully, after a century of successes and failures by American workers and their leaders, Mitchell's work can be intelligently assessed within the larger context of the labor movement.

By now Mitchell's meteoric rise to the presidency of the United Mine Workers of America (UMWA) has become the stuff of legends. Enduring a very difficult childhood, less than a grade-school education, and virtually no family support, Mitchell began working in the bituminous mines of Illinois and Colorado in his early teens. Returning to his home state of Illinois, Mitchell propelled himself into the officialdom of UMWA, District 12, and then to the UMWA vice-presidency in 1898. When UMWA president Michael Ratchford accepted a position with the United States Industrial Commission in 1898, he installed Mitchell as "acting president," a position outside of the union constitution, and then orchestrated his election to the presidency in January 1899 at the UMWA annual convention. In becoming

UMWA president, Mitchell had passed over several more-experienced and better-known leaders who surely resented this untested upstart and doubted seriously whether Mitchell would be up to this very difficult assignment. Mitchell would soon prove the doubters wrong.[4]

Prior to becoming UMWA president, Mitchell had spent his entire career in the soft-coal fields. Now, as leader of the union, his abilities, talents and ideas were a perfect match for the new situation in the bituminous industry. After years of conflict, the UMWA had signed a historic joint interstate contract with the mine operators of Illinois, Indiana, Ohio and western Pennsylvania, known as the Central Competitive Field (CCF). Following a bitter strike in 1897, the UMWA and the operators sat down and negotiated a contract establishing peaceful relations in the soft-coal mines. In particular, because the absence of monopolization and consolidation had promoted an intensely competitive and cutthroat environment among soft-coal producers, many had reluctantly agreed to recognize the UMWA, hoping that a strong union could help the operators rationalize the industry and, as far as possible, take labor costs out of competition.[5]

With the landmark contract of 1898 signed, Mitchell and the UMWA leadership needed to accomplish two major goals in the soft-coal fields. First, they must convince the restive rank-and-file miners that a new day in industrial relations had dawned and that some necessary changes were required. Contracts had to be followed religiously; the miners could no longer strike and take off work whenever they felt aggrieved. The agreement provided a process for resolving conflicts. Further, to enforce the contract on both miners and operators, union power had to be centralized in the national UMWA, the national officers and the national executive board. Districts, sub-districts and local unions had to surrender some of their autonomy to the national headquarters in the interest of constructing a powerful organization that could maintain the peace or fight the operators as conditions warranted.

Second, Mitchell and the UMWA were obligated to protect and solidify the interstate contract in the CCF by extending union authority into the adjacent unorganized fields of Pittsburgh, central Pennsylvania, Colorado and especially in the growing, low-cost fields of West Virginia. Only by organizing the miners in these areas could Mitchell prevent their owners from underselling the UMWA-recognized operators in the CCF. This called for a militant policy of organizing the miners into the UMWA umbrella.

The 28-year-old Mitchell displayed a masterful touch in solidifying his control of an unwieldy and undisciplined union. Prior to his presidency, most of the power resided within the various UMWA districts in bituminous, particularly District 6, Ohio, and District 12, Illinois. Mitchell's plan was to strengthen the authority of the national officials and then use this enhanced authority to build good relationships with compliant officials in those key districts. Once this authority was translated into solid gains at the bargaining table, the rest of the organizational structure would fall into place.

Centralization came about by Mitchell utilizing a variety of tactics, some of dubious constitutional and moral validity. He was given the power to create and direct essential strike funds only to those strikes approved by national officials. He assigned organizers to whatever coal fields he desired, frequently using them as cheerleaders for his plans and policies. He deftly managed the transactions of the annual national convention, making certain that there was a large turnout of delegates from districts favoring his leadership and placing his allies on key committees conducting the convention's business. He increased circulation of the UMWA Journal, imposing his imprimatur on the editorials, articles and letters that filled its pages. When he felt it necessary, Mitchell could really play hardball, discrediting his political opponents within the UMWA, as when he used union funds and unseemly methods to attack Patrick Dolan, president of District 5 in Pittsburgh.[6]

Yet, Mitchell's centralization drive did not destroy UMWA democracy. Districts retained a good deal of authority and Mitchell never had the national union assume control of districts, which would become common policy later. Mitchell increased the membership on the national executive board to provide for an elected representative from each district. During district and national conventions, his opponents freely castigated his policies and actions from the floor. His handling of a 1905 strike in Colorado called forth thunderous denunciation by socialists and others. Mitchell allowed William D. Haywood to address the 1908 national convention, Mitchell's last as UMWA president, when Haywood blasted the UMWA (and Mitchell's) policy of opposing sympathy strikes.[7] As in these two examples, Mitchell's opponents criticized him in front of hundreds of UMWA members, who, after hearing this criticism, responded by frequently approving his policies or following his recommendations. And while I will suggest that some of his later moves were costly to the UMWA, all of these decisions were ratified, in some fashion, by the UMWA rank and file or their representatives. Mitchell could be devious, shifty and unethical, but he was not a dictator. His control was personal, brought about by the persuasiveness of his arguments, enhanced by his prestige and success as a union leader. William B. Wilson discovered this when he ran as Mitchell's candidate in the 1908 UMWA presidential election only to lose out to Mitchell's rival, vice-president Tom L. Lewis.

From 1899 to 1903, Mitchell and UMWA made significant progress in protecting the interstate contract in the CCF by organizing adjacent nonunion fields. Mitchell was a firm believer in collective bargaining and the

trade agreement as the solution to the "labor problem." During the joint ses-
sions with the bituminous operators Mitchell was a superb bargainer, amass-
ing an incredible amount of statistics on every phase of coal production,
which he could recite by memory when making an argument on behalf of the
miners. When negotiations bogged down, he speeded things up. When the
operators refused to budge after the miners had made some concessions, he
would get tough and warn "that we have no expectation of discussing this
thing any further tonight unless a proposition is submitted by the operators."
If the owners tried to shift the blame for an impending breakdown in negotiations to the miners, Mitchell refused to accept it and retorted that "the operators must agree to give them [miners] that share of the profits they are
entitled to, otherwise the responsibility will rest on them and not on us. We
ask you, gentlemen, to divide those profits."[8]

Using the CCF agreement as a model, Mitchell was relentless in pushing
the UMWA into non-union territory. The UMWA extended the interstate
joint conference into the southwest, where District 14 (Kansas), District 21
(Arkansas and Indian Territory), and District 25 (Missouri) signed contracts
with operators, including several large anti-union railroads. Thousands of
miners were organized in District 2 (central Pennsylvania) and in District 8
(Alabama). UMWA membership approached 10,000 miners by 1903. New
districts were formed in Montana, British Columbia, Maryland, Michigan
and Kentucky.[9] Finally, and this has not been given the attention it deserves
in the standard accounts, Mitchell made a substantial and militant effort
during the 1902 anthracite strike to organize the very difficult coal fields in
West Virginia. Since this effort reveals the young, aggressive Mitchell at his
best, it merits a brief analysis and discussion.[10]

In late 1900, Mitchell began his organizing campaign in West Virginia by
assigning a large contingent of men to those coal fields. From that time on,
Mitchell and the UMWA poured more and more money and men into West
Virginia. The rationale for this was clear cut. Increasing tonnage of cheap,
non-union West Virginia coal was competing with union-produced coal of
the CCF, threatening harmonious relations between operators and miners.
Although Mitchell reported at the 1902 annual convention that the
UMWA had organized 80 local unions with some 5,000 members, this was
not nearly enough. A few weeks later, at the interstate convention with the
bituminous operators, the UMWA failed to win any wage increase for the
second consecutive year, the operators maintaining that they were losing
more and more markets to cheaper West Virginia coal. At the district level,
UMWA members were in a rebellious mood over the failure to win a wage
increase. Mitchell had to make a move in West Virginia. Knowing the difficulties that lie ahead, he did not hesitate to take the necessary action.

At the Hazelton convention, May 14–16, 1902, called to decide whether a temporary suspension in anthracite should be made permanent, Mitchell and UMWA secretary-treasurer William B. Wilson decided to take advantage of the general shortage of fuel in eastern markets to call a general strike in West Virginia on June 7. Mitchell sent vice-president Tom L. Lewis and his best organizers, including Thomas J. Haggerty and Mother Jones, to lead the strike.

How many of West Virginia's 33,000 miners struck is unclear. Mitchell later claimed that based on early telegrams he received, approximately 80% of the men responded and the prospects for a complete tie-up were encouraging. Unfortunately, this initial success did not last and the West Virginia strike ultimately was lost, except for miners on the Kanawha River in southern West Virginia, where contracts were signed with 7,000 miners giving them some of the conditions won by UMWA members in the CCF. The strike failed not because Mitchell and the UMWA were negligent in spending money and union resources or engaging in militant activity. The strike was lost due to several sweeping injunctions issued by federal and state courts that virtually denied the miners any form of strike activity, including any actions that interfered with the operation of the mines. Dozens of union officials and strike leaders, including Haggerty and Mother Jones, were jailed for some time. By late August, the strike was smashed except for the Kanawha field.[11]

I spend some time on this strike to demonstrate that Mitchell, during these early years, did champion militant and aggressive action. Throughout 1901 and 1902, until the strike fund was established for the striking anthracite mine workers, Mitchell spent more UMWA money, and stationed more organizers and officials in West Virginia than any other single district, including the entire anthracite field. In all, the UMWA spent almost $400,000 in West Virginia during 1902, a huge sum of money on one strike, and there were no complaints from the coal fields about the inadequacy of strike aid. Lack of effort and money did not lose the West Virginia strike. Mitchell gave it his best shot but the complete domination of the states' legal structure by the coal companies doomed the UMWA in West Virginia from 1902 and would continue to do so until the 1930s.

Mitchell's foray into the anthracite coal fields constituted part of this early organizing movement. Given his background experience and success in bituminous, it was only natural that he would use the same approach, building the UMWA among the anthracite mine workers until a collective bargaining relationship could be established with the anthracite operators. Mitchell carried the bituminous model into the hard-coal fields.

Mitchell began his campaign in anthracite in 1899 by putting down a challenge to his leadership by John Fahy, the most prominent UMWA official in hard-coal during the 1890s. Fahy had publicly criticized the national officials for ignoring the anthracite mine workers and he committed the cardinal sin of unionism by instructing several local unions to withhold the per capita tax from the national treasury. Mitchell seized upon this threat to his leadership to exert his authority and also take a first-hand look at the situation in anthracite prior to making a strike move. He called a convention of all UMWA members for Wilkes-Barre on August 24. Mitchell used this opportunity, attended by about 100 mine workers, to demonstrate his organizational skills and display his strong personality. According to his own account, he handled Fahy "without gloves" and rendered him the worst "turning down" of his life. Fahy completely capitulated to Mitchell, turned in the per capita tax and, on board the Mitchell train, was later elected president of newly formed District 9 in the lower anthracite fields.[12]

Throughout the remainder of 1899 and 1900, Mitchell cooperated with the district officials, providing organizers and national board members at their request. The officials of all three anthracite districts appeared before the national executive board in February, 1900, to discuss the situation. At this meeting Mitchell clearly wanted to strike at some point in the near future, but when two out of the three districts (District 1 in the minority) opposed a strike Mitchell postponed his plans until all three districts were ready to move in unison. In the meantime, Mitchell followed the bituminous pattern and instructed the district officials to invite the operators to meet them in a joint conference. The operators refused and events unfolded that led to the 1900 strike in anthracite.

Mitchell's brilliant management of the 1900 strike has been analyzed by several scholars, including myself, but let me underscore some key considerations.[13] From the beginning Mitchell believed that a region-wide strike was necessary in anthracite to establish the UMWA as a permanent organization there. He worked closely and harmoniously with district and local officials, keeping the union men on the national payroll and soliciting their recommendations for Slavic-speaking organizers. At times he personally interviewed potential organizers and he sent his best bituminous men to the hard-coal fields with orders to speak positively to the men, to abstain from name-calling and to treat the immigrants as equals. He was unwavering in his commitment to unionize the anthracite mine workers.[14]

John Mitchell made use of the press as no strike leader had before in the history of the United States labor movement. He forged alliances with religious leaders like Bishop Hoban of Scranton, Catholic priests like Father John Curran of Wilkes Barre and a host of local influential citizens. Despite some negative, private remarks about the anthracite men, he was always available to meet with average mine workers and he gave special consideration to the concerns of the immigrants. We know they responded by treating him like a hero.[15]

Finally, Mitchell took full advantage of the fall presidential campaign and election, the Republican Party's slogan of the full dinner pail and his contacts with Senator Mark Hanna, President McKinley's campaign manager, and an operator who had dealt with the UMWA through his bituminous mines in Ohio. Mitchell astutely utilized the political environment surrounding the election to extract the best deal he could from the operators before the election date, when this political pressure evaporated. He firmly believed that the settlement, which included a 10 percent advance, "does not correct many of the abuses under which the mine workers labor, but if accepted will give them encouragement and a big organization."[16] The mine workers resumed work on October 29, later designated as "Mitchell Day," a holiday in hard coal. The 1900 settlement was a crucial victory, but only the beginning of a movement whose goal was union recognition and a signed contract with the anthracite operators.

As a labor leader who put his faith in collective bargaining and signed contracts or the trade agreement, Mitchell used the same approach in anthracite that had worked so well in bituminous. Organize a substantial number of men into the UMWA, impress the operators with the businesslike nature of the union, its conservative, responsible leadership, its ability to control the rank and file, and its religious adherence to any agreement, all in the interest of industrial peace. Mitchell was no dummy. He knew that the situation in anthracite was vastly different than bituminous. He was well aware of how the railroads owned the coal companies, constituting a combination that did not need the UMWA to take wage rates and general labor costs out of competition, a primary role played by the UMWA in bituminous. Nonetheless, he envisioned that by bringing outside political and public pressure, combined with his conservative leadership of a union including a majority of mine workers, he could ultimately convince the operators that collective bargaining and union recognition were essential to running their mines. If they would not respond peacefully, he would force them to the table by closing down their mines.

In many ways, the 1902 strike constituted Mitchell's and the anthracite mine workers' finest hour. Yet, it also revealed the limitations of Mitchell's leadership and initiated his downward slide as president of the UMWA.

At the end of his long career, Samuel Gompers called the 1902 anthracite strike "the most important single event in the labor movement in the United States."[17] Much has been written about Mitchell's magnificent management of the strike and the steadfastness of the courageous mine workers. I would like to focus on some prominent features of Mitchell's leadership during the strike, perhaps gleaning some insight into why the settlement proved to be a double-edged sword.

One of the issues that arose during the strike was whether or not the bituminous miners should be called out in sympathy with the hard-coal mine workers.[18] From the start, Mitchell was unalterably opposed to such action. It would cause Mark Hanna, Ralph Easely of the National Civic Federation and other public figures to cease their efforts on behalf of the mine workers. It would risk alienating public support, which he had labored so hard to cultivate. Most importantly, a sympathy strike would break existing agreements and destroy all of his efforts and arguments for signing contracts. While Mitchell opposed a sympathy strike, he wrung all the political benefit possible by employing its threat as a "big stick" to wave over the heads of the operators and those forces working to bring about a strike settlement. Divorcing himself from a general strike, Mitchell privately informed Hanna that a resolution was introduced at the Hazelton convention of May 14–16, requesting that the striking miners in the Michigan and West Virginia districts join with the three anthracite districts and call for a special national convention to consider a general strike. (The UMWA constitution required five districts to call for a special national convention.) Mitchell told Hanna that this resolution was "railroaded through," when in reality it was introduced by a Mitchell ally and the UMWA president made no protest against its adoption. Mitchell also revealed to Hanna that he possessed the necessary petitions to call the special convention, but was delaying doing so in the hope that outside negotiations would produce something positive that might lead to a settlement. Continuing to pressure Hanna, he stated that while he would not break contracts, many bituminous miners not under contracts would cooperate with the anthracite strikers and furnish enough votes to call a sympathy strike. After delaying the special convention call for two months and extracting every possible consideration from a potential sympathy strike, Mitchell called the special convention and persuaded the delegates to adopt a relief fund for the anthracite strikers instead of conducting a sympathy strike. The relief fund provided financial support to carry on the anthracite strike.[19]

One of the most controversial issues of the strike involved union recognition, a part of the original demands formulated by the Shamokin convention of March 18. On April 26, Mitchell and the anthracite district officials met the operators for two days of negotiations during which the UMWA officials jettisoned many of the Shamokin demands until their final position included a wage increase of ten percent, a nine-hour day and the weighing of coal. When the Hazelton convention met May 14–16 to decide if the work stoppage should become permanent, union recognition was no longer a priority issue. During the strike industrialist Abram Hewitt publicly charged that union recognition and UMWA domination of the anthracite industry was Mitchell's real strike goal. Acting quickly to dispel this charge from the public arena, Mitchell replied that union recognition had never been the paramount issue of the strike. Rather, the mine workers were fighting for living wages and working conditions. Mitchell denied his oft-repeated hope for collective bargaining and recognition of the UMWA, similar to what had been achieved in bituminous, because he sincerely believed (perhaps rightly so) that the public would not suffer empty coal bins in sympathy with the strikers, for the primary purpose of forcing the operators to recognize the UMWA.[20] In jettisoning union recognition, Mitchell and the anthracite leadership were discarding the most potent weapon that the mine workers could employ in their struggle for fair and equitable treatment from the owners. Union recognition and the right to belong to a union were much more fundamental than any specific pay raise or reduction in hours. Mitchell learned this lesson in the post-1902 years, but for now the only hope for the UMWA in anthracite was to accept the Coal Strike Commission's award as a compromise victory, organize the non-union men, and prepare for the next round in 1906, when the commission's award and many bituminous contracts expired on the same date.[21]

In the meantime, the 1902 anthracite strike thrust national fame on the 32-year-old UMWA leader. He was besieged by newspaper people for interviews, by promoters for product endorsements, and by invitations to banquets and dinners. Traveling from Pennsylvania to Illinois, his train was greeted at every station by large crowds stretching to gain a glimpse of the mine workers' hero. People climbed on board to grab his hand and his appearance on the platform brought forth thunderous cheers. He dined with the governor of Illinois at his mansion amidst rumors that Mitchell would soon run for that office. With the assistance of Progressive writer Walter Weyl, who had helped Mitchell prepare for his testimony before the Coal Strike Commission, the UMWA leader authored several articles and a book, *Organized Labor*, which served as an oft-quoted treatment of American labor for several years. With the country riding the crest of an economic boom, Mitchell and the UMWA won substantial wage increases for the bituminous miners in the 1903 interstate conferences in the CCF and the southwest. In 1903 John Mitchell was the most popular and famous labor leader in the United States, if not the world.[22]

Unfortunately, 1903 was a turning point in Mitchell's union career. The fame and notoriety associated with the great 1902 strike changed Mitchell from an aggressive union leader to a successful union president concerned primarily with preserving and holding on to what had been won. While it is true that the qualities Mitchell displayed after 1902 had always been present in the early years, they were overshadowed by his willingness to build a strong union and use it as an instrument to organize coal miners and bring them out on strike whenever conciliation and arbitration failed to convince the operators to recognize and sign contracts with the UMWA. Mitchell's fame and notoriety, his association with wealthy businessmen, national politicians and other public figures, his infatuation with public praise as a conservative and cautious union leader, all dissipated whatever militancy the young union president possessed. Having constructed a mighty army of over 300,000 loyal miners who exalted his person, trusted his judgement and were willing to follow his leadership, Mitchell now refused to lead his troops to battle. Unwilling to take the risks essential to moving forward, Mitchell became obsessed with the haunting fear of defeat. A few examples will illustrate this.

During a 1903–1904 strike in Colorado that Mitchell had initiated, the UMWA president engineered the acceptance of a settlement by the northern Colorado miners while the southern Colorado miners remained on strike and were ultimately defeated. Although Mitchell and the UMWA spent almost $400,000 during this strike, he made several serious public relations blunders (of the kind that he had rarely made earlier). He spent several weeks sightseeing in Europe, traveling in luxury and dining with the anti-union industrialist Andrew Carnegie at his castle while the southern Colorado miners were being starved into submission. During the strike he made a perfunctory visit to Denver and spent most of the time talking to businessmen instead of visiting the strikers and their supporters in their coal camps. His absentee management of this important strike and the failure in southern Colorado left him open to intense criticism from UMWA members.[23]

A much more ominous development took place in 1904. Instead of striking when the CCF operators proposed a five and a half percent wage reduction, Mitchell outmaneuvered a special convention of bituminous miners which voted against the wage cut and convinced the delegates at the last minute to agree to a referendum vote of all soft-coal miners whose contracts were expiring. Then Mitchell utilized all of the UMWA resources to convince the miners to vote for the wage cut, which they did by a vote of 102,026 to 67,951. Although he may have sincerely believed that a strike would fail, the wage cut caused huge problems for the UMWA. While the CCF operators reduced the wages by the agreed amount, operators in surrounding coal fields where the UMWA was beginning to make inroads saw the reduction as a sign of weakness, and started instituting larger wage cuts and breaking signed contracts. The wage reduction cost Mitchell and the UMWA thousands of members in the soft-coal fields. Criticism mounted of Mitchell and the union leadership. The miners were restless and angry.[24]

The setbacks suffered by Mitchell and the UMWA in 1904 might have been forgotten had the union leadership taken advantage of the opportunities presented in 1906 when the contracts of many bituminous miners as well as the Anthracite Strike Commission's Award expired on March 31. Mitchell had preached about this contingency in 1904 while urging the soft-coal miners to accept the wage cut. Throughout much of 1905 he rebuilt the UMWA, sending organizers into the non-union fields of District 5, Pittsburgh, and District 2, central Pennsylvania. He personally addressed a series of mass meetings with miners throughout the CCF. Much of the summer was spent among the anthracite mine workers where he addressed 65 rallies before 350,000 people, reiterating the demands of formal UMWA recognition and the eight-hour day. At the end of his anthracite tour Mitchell boasted of organizing 60,000 to 70,000 men in three months. A militant-sounding Mitchell address at the 1906 annual UMWA convention projected an image of a general readying his troops for the coming battles.[25]

In February and March, 1906, Mitchell conducted negotiations simultaneously with the bituminous and anthracite operators. After days of bargaining, the soft-coal owners offered only a renewal of the 1904 contract, a proposal angrily rejected by Mitchell and the UMWA. A strike in bituminous on April 1 seemed a certainty. In the meantime, Mitchell faced a significant internal challenge from the president of District 5, Pat Dolan, who had voted to accept the operators' offer and had publicly criticized Mitchell as a dictator who had no regard for the public interest and was willing to bring on an industrial confrontation not warranted by mining conditions. Many newspapers sided with Dolan, criticizing Mitchell for his irresponsible and radical position. Although Dolan was removed from office by a convention of District 5 miners, his actions pressured Mitchell to achieve some sort of victory in bituminous without a general strike.

This led Mitchell to conduct a series of secret negotiations with several leading bituminous operators, including Francis Robbins of the huge Pittsburgh Coal Company. These owners agreed to restore the 1903 contract. Many operators, however, refused to go along and so Mitchell and most of the UMWA leadership convinced the delegates attending a special national convention to accept district settlements based on the 1903 agreement instead of having the CCF miners and the southwestern fields strike in unison. Pressured by the press that had previously lionized him and in accord with his own genuine fears of a national bituminous walk-out, Mitchell squandered an opportunity that he had prepared the miners to seize. District settlements were a disaster. Although thousands of miners received a wage increase, the interstate movement so important to the UMWA was demolished. District settlements pitted miner against miner, wrecking the sense of solidarity that had been building since the 1904 debacle. Demoralization and dissatisfaction were rife throughout the soft-coal fields.[26]

In similar fashion, Mitchell retreated from the coming battle in anthracite. On December 14, 1905, a convention of anthracite mine workers met at Shamokin and formulated their demands in executive session. Mitchell held the anthracite cards tight to his chest. He refused to discuss the mine workers' demands with the press. At the annual UMWA convention in January, 1906, the issues important to the anthracite mine workers received little attention by the delegates. So, too, at the special national convention in March, very little was said about the anthracite negotiations despite the fact that many anthracite leaders wanted to air out their issues with their bituminous brothers and plot a common course of action. Mitchell kept the two sets of negotiations completely separate and conducted each in a shroud of secrecy and with backroom maneuvers.[27]

Mitchell and the anthracite leaders met the operators for the first time face-to-face on February 15, 1906. Their demands included an eight-hour day, uniform wages for the same class of labor, a scale of wages for deadwork,* a wage increase, coal paid by weight when practicable, reorganization of the Board of Conciliation, and a one-year contract with union recognition. The operators rejected everything, merely offering to extend the Anthracite Strike Commission's award for another three years. Mitchell engaged in the same kind of covert moves that he was using in bituminous. He stated privately that while the mine workers would strike rather than renew the award, if the operators would grant any favorable concessions he would induce the men to withdraw many of their demands. He tried to have intermediaries arrange a private meeting with himself and George Baer. This failed and on April 1, approximately 140,000 mine workers began what Mitchell termed a "suspension" of work. After several proposals involving various forms of arbitration were rejected by both parties, Mitchell made his final offer: an advance of ten cents per ton upon the total production of anthracite coal to the wages of all workers. When the operators rejected this final proposal, a convention of anthracite UMWA delegates, following the recommendation of Mitchell and the anthracite UMWA leadership, voted to acccept a renewal of the award, end Mitchell's "suspension" and return to work. Although Mitchell tried to paint the settlement as a victory, the mine workers thought otherwise. By year's end UMWA membership in anthracite had declined from 80,000 to 30,000 men.[28]

In three short years, the UMWA went from a militant and aggressive union of over 300,000 coal miners to an organization that was in retreat, weakened by the settlements of 1904 and 1906. At the UMWA annual convention in 1907, almost 100,000 coal miners had disappeared from the union rolls. Only 580 delegates instead of the usual 1,200 attended this gathering. Discontent with the UMWA (much less so with Mitchell) was extensive throughout the coal fields.[29]

Was John Mitchell solely to blame for this tragic state of affairs? Of

---

*   Work necessary before the vein of coal became accessible.

course not. Mitchell's policies and decisions were ratified in one form or another by the UMWA leadership and the rank and file. Furthermore, Mitchell genuinely believed that his policies were appropriate for the environment
within which the UMWA had to maneuver. Thus the 1904 wage cut and
the 1906 district settlements in bituminous were the best that could be won
without a national strike, which Mitchell felt would end in defeat. Likewise,
the 1906 settlement in anthracite was the only option without continuing
the so-called "suspension." From experience Mitchell knew that strikes, especially large ones, carried no guarantee of success. Nothing injured a union
more than a failed strike.[30]

While Mitchell is not solely to blame for the decline of the UMWA, he
must bear ultimate responsibility. What really happened, I suggest, is that
success, especially that of the 1902 strike, proved to be the undoing of John
Mitchell. During the years 1899 to 1902, Mitchell earned the loyalty and
trust of coal miners everywhere by exercising his leadership skills and his personal qualities to advance their cause in numerous ways. Together Mitchell
and the rank and file built the UMWA into a powerful weapon for fairness
and justice in the coal fields. Yet the success of Mitchell and the union only
whetted the coal miners' appetite for more since there remained thousands
of unorganized men. Mitchell's leadership and the union's victories awak-
ened the coal miners to a deep sense of their potential power. They were
willing to carry the struggle onward.

Something happened to Mitchell after the 1902 strike. He became transformed from a union leader to a national labor spokesman. He wrote and
spoke forcefully for collective bargaining, the trade agreement and unionism.
But when it came to leading coal miners, he put too much faith in politicians, businessmen and public figures in behind-the-scenes negotiations. He
came to rely too much on public approval and press support before making a
move. He was afraid to take risks essential to any victory. Having created a
powerful army, he feared committing it to all-out battle. He was terrified of
failure. All of these tendencies were present in the young Mitchell, but the
1902 strike and the fame that came with it pushed these propensities center
stage.

Along the way John Mitchell lost sight of the fact that collective bargaining and signed contracts could oftentimes be won only by bitter and costly
strikes waged by the miners and their leaders. UMWA success in the CCF
came only after a coordinated campaign of miners' solidarity was climaxed
by a national strike. The 1906 district settlements destroyed this solidarity.
Union recognition in anthracite was the one weapon that would enable the
mine workers to achieve their goals. The operators would reluctantly agree
to union recognition only after the mine workers made it clear that without
the union the mines would not yield coal. The mine workers understood this

and were willing to fight in 1906. Mitchell was not. While he remained their personal hero, his union, the UMWA would suffer tough times for another decade until the mine workers ignored the UMWA leadership and forged their own union.[31]

Let me close this paper by paraphrasing something I wrote in a review of Craig Phelan's fine biography of Mitchell. The real tragedy of Mitchell's leadership of the UMWA is not about what he accomplished, for he accomplished much in a short time. Rather, given his talent, popularity and ability, the tragedy is what might have been.

Notes

1. Robert J. Cornell, *The Anthracite Coal Strike of 1902* (Washington, DC: The Catholic University of America Press, 1957).

2. The standard accounts of anthracite unionism are Harold Aurand, *From the Molly Maguires to the United Mine Workers: The Social Ecology of an Industrial Union, 1869–1897* (Philadelphia: Temple University Press, 1971), Perry Blatz, *Democratic Miners: Work and Labor Relations in the Anthracite Coal Industry, 1875–1925* (Albany: State University of New York Press, 1994), Maier B. Fox, *United We Stand: The United Mine Workers of America, 1890–1900* (Washington, DC: United Mine Workers of America, 1990), and Donald Miller and Richard E. Sharpless, *The Kingdom of Coal: Work, Enterprise and Ethnic Communities in the Mine Fields* (Philadelphia, University of Pennsylvania Press, 1985). An excellent collection of essays on the United Mine Workers of America is John Laslett, ed., *The United Mine Workers of America: A Model of Industrial Solidarity* (University Park: The Pennsylvania State University Press, 1996).

3. Joseph M. Gowaskie, "John Mitchell: A Study in Leadership," Ph.D. dissertation, The Catholic University of America, 1968, and Craig Phelan, *Divided Loyalties: The Public and Private Life of Labor Leader John Mitchell* (Albany: State University of New York Press, 1994). See also the article by James O. Morris which investigates Mitchell's financial dealings and raised serious questions about his ethical conduct and his integrity, "The Acquisitive Spirit of John Mitchell, UMW President (1899– 1908)," *Labor History* 20 (Winter, 1979), 5–43.

4. These early years are in Gowaskie, Chapters 1 and 2 and Phelan, *Divided Loyalties*, Chapter 1.

5. Joseph M. Gowaskie, "From Conflict to Cooperation: John Mitchell and Bituminous Coal Operators," *The Historian* 38 (August, 1976), 669–88.

6. Gowaskie, "Mitchell," 26–76; Phelan, *Divided Loyalties*, Chapter 2.

7. The Colorado strike and Haywood's appearance is covered in Gowaskie "Mitchell," 257–71, 355–57, and Phelan, *Divided Loyalties*, 212–25 and 355–57. Phelan is quite critical of Mitchell's centralization actions. See 63–76.

8. On Mitchell as negotiator see Gowaskie, "Mitchell," 82–84; Phelan, *Divided Loyalties*, 85–87.

9. Gowaskie "Mitchell," 192–93. For an excellent summary of Mitchell's union career see Craig Phelan, "John Mitchell and the Politics of the Trade Agreement, 1898– 1917," in Laslett, ed., *The United Mine Workers of America*, 72–103.

10. The West Virginia strike is treated in Gowaskie, "Mitchell," Chapter 4.

11. Ibid., 144–45.

12. Gowaskie, "Mitchell," 47–54; Blatz, *Democratic Miners*, 66–67; Phelan, *Divided Loyalties*, 95–98.

13. Cornell, *Strike of 1902*, Chapter 2; Blatz, *Democratic Miners*, Chapter 4; Phelan, *Divided Loyalties*, Chapter 3; and "The Making of a Labor Union Leader: John

Mitchell and the Anthracite Strike of 1990," *Pennsylvania History*, 63 (Winter, 1996), 53–77.

14. Gowaskie, "Mitchell," 88–103.

15. Phelan, "John Mitchell," 83, accuses Mitchell of using "ethnic slurs" like "cattle" to describe the anthracite mine workers. This is a bit harsh. Victor R. Greene's book *The Slavic Community on Strike: Immigrant Labor in Pennsylvania Anthracite* (Notre Dame: University of Notre Dame Press, 1968), 198–203, gives Mitchell high marks for his efforts. Blatz, *Democratic Miners*, Chapters 4–6 is also more positive about Mitchell's relations with the immigrants. See also Joseph Gowaskie, "Charisma in the Coal Fields: John Mitchell and the Anthracite Mine Workers, 1899–1902," *Proceedings of the Canal History and Technology Symposium IV*, Anthracite Issue (Easton, PA: Canal History and Technology Press, 1985), 131–46.

16. Gowaskie, "Mitchell," 96.

17. Quoted in Edmund Morris, *Theodore Rex* (New York: Random House, 2001), 624, n. 169.

18. Cornell, *Strike of 1902*, 100–19; Gowaskie, "Mitchell," 170–80; Blatz, *Democratic Miners*, 134–35; Phelan, *Divided Loyalties*, 167–74.

19. Gowaskie, "Mitchell," 179–80.

20. Gowaskie, "Mitchell," 165.

21. For negative assessments of the 1902 strike settlement see Joe Gowaskie, "John Mitchell and the Anthracite Mine Workers: Leadership Conservatism and Rank-and-File Militancy," *Labor History* 27 (Winter, 1985–86), 54–83 and Phelan, *Divided Loyalties*, 185–88. Blatz, *Democratic Miners*, 139–40 and Cornell, *Strike of 1902*, 234–35 are more favorable.

22. Gowaskie, "Mitchell," 190–93; Phelan, *Divided Loyalties*, 208–12.

23. Gowaskie, "Mitchell," 257–71; Phelan, *Divided Loyalties*, 212–25. See also Priscilla Long, *Where the Sun Never Shines: A History of America's Bloody Coal Industry* (New York: Paragon House, 1989), Chapter 10.

24. Gowaskie, "Mitchell," 234–52. Mitchell later admitted he made a mistake in agreeing to the wage reduction. 286 n.18. See also Phelan, *Divided Loyalties*, 225–34.

25. Gowaskie, "Mitchell," 279–87, and "Leadership Conservatism," 71–73. See also Blatz, *Democratic Miners*, 185–87.

26. The bituminous negotiations are covered in Gowaskie, "Mitchell," 292–325, 343–45; Phelan, *Divided Loyalties*, 260–75, 285–87.

27. Gowaskie, "Mitchell," 325–35 and "Leadership Conservatism," 73–76; Phelan, *Divided Loyalties*, 274–84; Blatz, *Democratic Miners*, 188–92.

28. Gowaskie, "Mitchell," 329–42; Phelan, *Divided Loyalties*, 278–84; Blatz, *Democratic Miners*, 192–204.

29. Gowaskie, "Mitchell," 348; Phelan, *Divided Loyalties*, 286.

30. Phelan, *Divided Loyalties*, 289, suggests that a national strike in anthracite and bituminous might have been successful. Blatz, *Democratic Miners*, 203, argues that such a strike would likely have failed because of all the obstacles confronting it.

31. Blatz, *Democratic Miners*, Chapter 9. See also Joe Gowaskie, "Petty Grievances and Button Strikes: The Anthracite Mine Workers Forge a Union," unpublished paper delivered at the Centennial Conference of the United Mine Workers of America, Pennsylvania State University, October 1990.

BIOGRAPHICAL NOTES

RICHARD HEALEY is currently professor of geography at the University of Portsmouth in England. He obtained his undergraduate and doctoral degrees from the University of Cambridge and taught at the University of Edinburgh for 15 years before moving to Portsmouth. His research interests include the historical geography of industrial development in the northeast United States, with particular reference to the coal mining, iron and railroad industries; computer modeling of regional industrial development and the use of geographic information science methods for the management and analysis of historical data resources. He is currently completing a book on the growth of the Pennsylvanian anthracite coal industry between the Civil War and the 1902 Coal Strike.

JOE GOWASKIE is a professor of history at Rider University. He has published essays and reviews in *The Historian*, *The History Teacher*, *Pennsylvania History*, *Labor History*, and the *Journal of American History*. He has been active in the faculty union, Rider University AAUP, where he served as president. As an undergraduate, he studied under Robert J. Cornell, author of *The Anthracite Coal Strike of 1902*, and did his doctoral dissertation on John Mitchell at the Catholic University of America. He teaches courses in U.S. History and World History and is a recipient of the Rider University Distinguished Teaching Award. He is an avid fan of the Green Bay Packers, having worked at Lambeau Field during his undergraduate years.

ROBERT JANOSOV is a professor of history at Luzerne County Community College. He holds a bachelor of arts degree from King's College, and a master of arts degree from Niagara University. He served as a member of the Pennsylvania Historic Preservation Board from 1993 to 1997. He has served as a board member and president of the Wyoming Historical & Geological Society. He is president of GRIT, Inc., the non-profit corporation that built and operates Washington Square Apartments for the elderly in Wilkes-Barre. Professor Janosov has been researching, lecturing, and publishing the industrial heritage of northeastern Pennsylvania's anthracite region for twenty years. Along with numerous articles, he published *A Preliminary Survey of Wyoming Valley's Historic Anthracite Sites* in 1992. His book, *Cold & Gold from the Poconos: A History of the Stegmaier Brewery, Wilkes-Barre, Pa*, was published in 1997. He has served as a historical consultant for the United States Department of the Interior, the National Park Service, the Pennsylvania Bureau of Historic Preservation, the Luzerne County Office of Community Development, the Delaware and Lehigh National Heritage Corridor, the Housing Development Corporation of Northeastern Pennsylvania, the Borough of Bear Creek Village, the City of Wilkes-Barre, the Wyoming Monument Association, St. Gabriel's Catholic parish in Hazleton, and Catholic Social Services. As a consultant he specializes in researching and writing Historic Survey Reports, Section 106 Reports, and National Register Nominations.

JOSEPH P. MCKERNS is a professor of journalism and communication at the Ohio State University. His area of research specialization is the history of news media in the United States. In 2002 he was designated a Scholar-in-Residence at the Anthracite Heritage Museum in Scranton by the Pennsylvania Historical and Museum Commission. He is a native of Shenandoah, and a descendant of Irish and Polish coal miners and railroad workers.

LANCE E. METZ is the historian for the National Canal Museum in Easton, Pennsylvania. He has a B.A. in history from Moravian College, Bethlehem, an M.A. in history from the University of Maine at Orono, and completed the museum studies program at Lehigh University. He created the Center for Canal History and Technology and its publication program in 1981, and has acquired important collections for the National Canal Museum's archives. Among his many published works are "An Examination of the Crellin Letters," in *Canal History and Technology Proceedings*, Volume I, 1982; *Robert H. Sayre: Engineer, Entrepreneur and Humanist* (1985); *Charles M. Schwab: Man of Industry and Culture* (1986); *John Fritz: His Role in the Rise of the American Steel Industry* (1987); and "The Prosecution of the Molly Maguires in Carbon County, Pa." in *Canal History and Technology Proceedings*, Volume XIX, 2000. Metz has co-authored numerous papers and books on industrial and canal history, and has conducted several oral history projects, most notably the ongoing program to record the memories of retired workers on America's last towpath canal. He is a consultant for many canal-related preservation and restoration projects, has prepared 31 nominations to the National Register of Historic Places, and has served as the historian for several HAER surveys of industrial plants.

ROBERT P. WOLENSKY is a professor of sociology and co-director of the Center for the Small City at the University of Wisconsin-Stevens Point. He has co-authored two books with his brother, Ken, and daughter, Nicole: *The Knox Mine Disaster: The Final Years of the Northern Anthracite Industry and the Effort to Rebuild a Regional Economy* (Pennsylvania Historical and Museum Commission, 1999), and *Fighting for the Union Label: The Women's Garment Industry and the ILGWU in Pennsylvania* (Penn State Press, 2002). He was a scholar-in-residence for the Pennsylvania Historical and Museum Commission in 1995, and will be a visiting professor at Wilkes University during fall 2002, and a visiting fellow at the Center for 21st Century Studies at the University of Wisconsin–Milwaukee in spring 2003. He is currently writing a book on the subcontracting and leasing of mineral rights in the northern anthracite field.